UNLOCK YOUR
LEADERSHIP

SECRETS & STRAIGHT ANSWERS ON
STANDING OUT, MOVING UP, AND GETTING AHEAD
AS THE LEADER YOU REALLY ARE

DAMARIS PATTERSON PRICE

ISBN 978-1-54398-871-0 (print)
ISBN 978-1-54398-872-7 (ebook)
Working River Leadership Consulting
8984 Darrow Road, Suite 2-221
Twinsburg OH 44087
United States
www.workingriver.com

For David and Sophia

Contents

Acknowledgments

To Judith Bradle, Jared Brown, Felicia Davis, Jennifer Barker Edwards, Michael Konesky, Erin Clymer Lessard, Tanya Loncar, Alyson Lyon, Brooke Moore, Kris Nunn, Tom Rosenak, and Don Zirkle: Thank you for your friendship, faith, fussing, and feedback. Thank you for the prodding, patience, and impatience. Thank you for your support, your shoulders, your eyes, your expertise, and your cheerleading. Know that it all inspired me to do my best work.

To Lisa Gaynier, Herb Stevenson, Dr. B (Phil Belzunce), and the Cleveland State University Diversity Management Program and Gestalt Institute of Cleveland communities: thank you for inspiring me to develop my own unique voice around using oneself well at work and in the world.

To my clients, who trusted me enough to show me their dreams and challenges, while allowing me to bear witness to their transformation, right before my eyes: thank you for inspiring this work.

To my first and most beloved teacher, Victoria Patterson: thank you, Mom, for your ever-present witticisms through which you passed on your wisdom and inspired my journey. You have one for every occasion. With pride, I find myself sounding more and more like you every day.

Author's Note

I am an executive coach and leadership development facilitator, which is to say that I get to help professionals and managers grow their leader-craft so that they can drive great business results with and through their people. In my relationships with my clients, their confidentiality is paramount. However, with permission, and because I knew they could bring this work to life, I used some of their stories, which are deeply relatable and rich with teachable moments. To protect my clients' privacy, the names, genders, roles, and circumstances reflected in the anecdotes have been altered and disguised. Many of the narratives are several stories aggregated into composite case studies to illustrate particular challenges with laser focus. But all are authentic and based on actual experiences to give you, the reader, the benefit of their learning and the knowledge that, on this journey, you are not alone.

Introduction

This work began with the questions:

Why am I not getting ahead?

What in the world is my boss talking about when she says I'm *not ready* to move up?

Why am I getting passed over when I see people who aren't any smarter than I am getting promoted?

When am I going to get a straight answer on what my manager means when he tells me to *step up and lead*?

I have experience; but why isn't it proof that I'm ready for the next level?

What's *really* going on?

Who do they think they are—these people who are deciding whether I'm *good enough*?

What's wrong with them?

What's wrong with me?

Why not me?

Anxious, pained, frustrated, and confused: a variety of people have presented the same problem to me in a variety of ways. But in my mind, it all boils down to the same truth: the moment you realize the people at your organization don't see it in you—it, the x factor, the leadership material; the thing that defines you as a long-term and bankable investment for your organization; the thing that holds you up as a high-potential employee and promotable; the thing that tells them you're ready for what's next at work. So, why don't they see these things in you, and what can you do about it? Those are questions that deserve answers. And answers are what we are here to explore. I call them answers; however, for those of you without the benefit of a mentor, sponsor, or coach, they are secrets, the insider knowledge you may otherwise never have the opportunity to learn. And as the saying goes: what you don't know can hurt you.

What This Book Is About

This book is about demonstrating your readiness for what's next at work. *What's next* could be a promotion or an invitation to sit on high visibility committees. *What's next* could mean being your department's much respected go-to person or getting the plum assignments. Whatever *what's next* means to you, how to get there is the tricky part. How to get there can be the mysterious part. Without the right support, how to get there can be the frustrating part. And how to get there is what this book is all about.

This book is about discovering your unique brand of leadership—and leveraging it to grow your career. Advancement. Moving up. Promotion. Taking on more responsibility.

Getting ahead. People call the means of their career climb by many different names—and at the core of all of them, is leadership. Any book about stepping up at work—formally or informally—is a book about leadership, or it should be. Management or not, no matter what the next-level role is or what your organization calls it, it is a step into a higher degree of leadership. That's the first lesson. To be promotable, you must be seen as a leader. Period. Full stop.

This book is not about management. Management—or the oversight of people, processes, and production—is just *one* function of *some* leaders. Organizations hope their managers will lead, but to be a leader, you need not have a management title because leadership is something else entirely. Leadership is not married to hierarchy, an organizational chart, or formal authority over a team. It's a different animal, with more depth, breadth, and impact. I've known people who were little more than the boss of the applesauce, and yet they proved to be outstanding leaders. And I've known some vice presidents, executives, and Grand Poobahs—all with high-powered management titles, and not one of them could lead themselves, or anyone else, around a corner.

This book is about what leadership is—and more importantly, what it does. But as you will discover, what leadership is can be frustratingly resistant to fitting into a nice, neat box. From antiquity forward, I can find, without any effort at all, stabs at what it is. Some leadership experts define it with adjectives or outcomes. Others use flowery and esoteric prose. But none of them seem to satisfy a simple question I know a lot of people are asking: What does someone need to do to be seen as a leader at work? Thus, the *leadership* we will discuss here will focus on the particular characteristics and pragmatic attributes organizations look for when they're looking for leaders. This book is about what your organization needs to see in you to recognize the leader you really are, as well as your readiness to handle what's next for you at work. We will discuss the walk, talk, and insights of someone who is next-level ready, high potential, someone who is leadership material, someone who is promotable, someone who is ready to lead.

This book will also deal honestly with why your leadership ability hasn't been as evident as it could be. We will delve into why the decision makers in your organization aren't thinking of you when they think of leadership. And who are "they"? This book will discuss that too—who the "theys" are—those mysterious individuals in your organization who decide whether you have earned enough influence, can inspire followership, and can trigger and accelerate positive results. But in the truest sense, this book is about you, what is masking your leadership capabilities, and what is holding you back from being your best self at work.

Whether you are an individual contributor, an internal consultant, a manager of projects or processes, a manager of people, or an established manager of multiple teams, this book will discuss how to lead in a way that is evident and obvious for others to feel, recognize, trust, appreciate, and reward. It will highlight strategies and tools that will transform and upgrade your daily walk and talk, as well as your thinking. The focus is on you as leadership material, powered with insights and strategies, coming out of hiding to reveal the leader you really are. Our conversation will demystify what has been in the way of the leadership career you want. The process will open your access to insider knowledge on what evident leadership actually looks like. And the final outcome? You being equipped to pursue the roles and opportunities you want at work with more confidence. If any of these statements reflect what you've been looking for, keep reading.

Getting the Most from This Experience

As I write this, it is important to me, as it is in my practice, to favor the pragmatic and real world over the academic and theoretical. So, here is an actionable tip from the start. As you move through the content and concepts, I invite you to engage in the Strategic Reflection exercises, through which you will talk to yourself—*about yourself* and what you are discovering along this journey. These coaching questions that are peppered throughout the content are designed to provide opportunities for you to pause and reflect in a way that stretches or challenges your current thinking. In my experience, when you have finished, what you will have learned about you *from you* will prove to be among the most valuable lessons of all. Look, here's one now...

Strategic Reflection No. 1

You have started down the path of a development journey that will result in you being able to pursue next-level roles and opportunities with more savvy and confidence. Think about that end state and the person you want to be after this experience. Once you emerge on the other side of this process, what do you want to have changed? What do you want to be different from today? In the space provided, list three shifts you want to see along the way. Identify changes that are within your control to influence, even though you may not yet know how. List what you will see more or less of as you approach a successful outcome. Lastly, to help these shifts take shape, note how you will help yourself stay the course. How will you keep yourself accountable and on the path? Here's an example.

Desired Shift: I don't want to be afraid to go after the roles I want at work. I want to pursue opportunities at work with more confidence.

Success Looks Like: I'll know the change is happening when I feel more surefooted going after next-level positions. I'll be using more strategy (and less wishful thinking). I'll be less afraid. And I'll know what to do in between promotions to get and keep myself ready.

To Help Myself Deliver: The Strategic Reflections—I'll use them to track what I'm learning as I go through the book. I'm going to write down what I'm really thinking to see if anything unexpected comes up. My friend and I have also agreed to go through this together. I'm more likely to follow-through with him as an accountability partner.

Desired Shift:

_____

_____

_____

_____

_____

_____

Success Looks Like:

_____

_____

_____

_____

_____

To Help Myself Deliver:

_____

_____

_____

_____

_____

You, Me, and We

As I wrote this book, I pictured you sitting here as one of my coaching clients, people who engage me to help them, through incremental and unfolding self-discovery, resolve a career challenge or advance their professional aspirations. It's with that image in my head that I wrote, working hard to show up, speak, and coach just as I would if you and I were sharing the same space. In these pages, I hope you get a true sense of who I am, my voice, my culture, my experience, my mistakes—and even, far too often, my mom. I couldn't help it; sometimes her famous proverbs just fit. Promise to never tell her I quoted her, though; as she'd like that way too much.

With only the ability to imagine who you might be, I will make a few assumptions. I will assume you are a strong performer whose work meets or exceeds your organization's expectations. You may want to be promoted into a management role, ascend into a higher level of management, or perhaps you just want to be elevated and respected as a thought leader, the go-to person, or a senior-level and specialized expert. Whether your career success story comes with a formal title or not, you're pretty clear on what you want. You only need a little help on the *how*.

I hope you experience this book as practical and easy to digest, just as if we were sitting together in conversation, but our coaching relationship does have its limitations. I have no general or specific knowledge of the organization for which you work, or its hiring or promotion practices. The concepts and strategies in this book are based on my nearly thirty years of corporate human resources and executive coaching experience in a variety of industries and domains. Although this book provides many of the same insights and tools that I share in my private coaching practice, there are several factors, both within and outside of your control, which can influence your ability to move up and around in an organization, so I cannot make any guarantees. No one ever can. However, this book will share many of the critical elements of recognizable leadership, as well as the methodologies that enable you to demonstrate them at work. In the end, it's you who has to step up and do the doing, but the conversation you and I are about to have will certainly point the way.

On a Personal Note

I've spent the majority of my career in the business of developing people, and I have loved every minute of it. However, during that time, I've noticed something that deeply disturbs me. Compared to all who want, need, and deserve it, surprisingly few people ever get a chance at effective and focused career coaching and leadership development. In the earlier days of my chosen field when I only aspired to do what I am so fortunate to be doing now, I needed leadership development. I needed it badly. And I was lucky. Mentoring and good managers for me were abundant. Unfortunately for them, my mentors and coaches didn't realize what a mess they were getting themselves into by taking my sophomoric and hardheaded self under their wings. By the time they figured it out, it was too late. I stuck to them like cold on ice, whereas they tolerated me. Although it was painful for everyone, they endured, and I learned. I'm still learning. And I'm forever in their debt.

For many people in need of leadership development, however, the message is, "Oh, you want to get ahead at work? Terrific! Hope you work that out!" And most do; they work it out—but not before riding the gauntlet of trial and error. Absent a supportive manager, mentor, or coach, learning the craft of leading means learning it the hard way, and often on your own. How many more great leaders would there be in the world if people only knew how, if they only had a partner on that journey?

This is my opportunity to pay back what others so generously gave to me. On this leg of your journey, I want to be your partner. So let me be the first to congratulate you on your decision to advance your career success story! It's one of the most critical decisions you can make and one that can positively reverberate through all parts of your life. In the marketplace, there are many career development products to choose from, available in a variety of shapes, sizes, and philosophies. Know that I appreciate that you chose this one to help you take these all-important steps, and I thank you for choosing to take them with me.

—*Damaris Patterson Price*

PART I

YOUR LEADERSHIP LOCKED

*"It would be too easy to say that I feel invisible.
Instead, I feel painfully visible, but entirely ignored."*

—*David Levithan,*
author and editor

They can't see you: the leader you really are.
All you've experienced, all you want to learn, all you
want to give, is hidden in plain sight.

Chapter 1

CONFESSIONS OF A CORPORATE "HRIAN"

The truth about the path to leadership at work

LET'S NOT BEAT around the bush because we both know why you're here: you want to be promoted into leadership. You want to be lifted to the next level. You want to be respected as the team's thought leader and go-to person. You want to be followed. You want to be listened to. You want to cause things to happen. You want to be invited. You want them to see you, and, while doing so, you want them to see a leader. Understood. Now, where's the first place you go? Most employees who want to fast track their careers toward leadership roles go to their boss. The luckiest among you have nurturing managers who have long identified your potential—perhaps even before you did—and have been grooming you, whether you realized it or not. Equally lucky are those among you who find your managers open and receptive when you approach them with your aspirations for next-level growth. They are responsive to your expressed interests and start walking with you on the road that leads to you being at the right place, at the right time, with the right skills when the lightning bolt of opportunity strikes. But for many without access to a nurturing guide, building your repute as a leader is lonely and mysterious work.

Throughout my years of coaching, I've heard many clients report feeling as if invisible and powerful forces were at work as they chased their next-level dream. Some of those forces seemed aligned with their aspirations to move up, whereas others seemed to be opposed. That's when the paranoia would begin: a feeling that, at worst, the deck was stacked against them and, at best, a promotion process that should be fairly black and white was much more complicated than they ever imagined. The truth was, and is, the same: most of these people aren't paranoid, and neither are you. With nearly three decades of experience in the people development business, I'm telling you that what you sense is real. There *are* forces and little-known processes influencing the paths toward leadership.

But be encouraged. Although these forces and realities deserve your respect, they are not something to fear. Instead, study them, as we will. Understand why and how they operate, and how to operate with them, and you exponentially increase your chances of managing your career to arrive in a good place. But if you ignore them, you won't get very far at all. The sad fact is that some employees have to go it alone. They have to make their own luck—and their own development plans. For those of you pursuing leadership opportunities on your own, for those of you supplementing the generous guidance of others, and for those of you who are here to sharpen your confidence and competitive edge, let's begin. But first, we'll need to go to church.

Behind the HRian Curtain

I am the product of a career spent in Human Resources (HR). And one thing I know for sure is, your average HR department is severely underrated and scarcely understood. HR departments are not organizational profit centers; that is, we don't make money for the company, we consume it, and we are often seen as a bland and fiscally inconsequential shared service of the enterprise. But what HR lacks in revenue generation, it makes up for in influence. If the organization is a community, HR is its church. The sacred keep of the organization's values, laws, social norms, and belief system, just like a house of worship, HR is the caretaker of the organization's philosophical ideology, with a reach that spans the entire enterprise. All organizations have a culture—a shared understanding of how the organization works, a shared knowing of right and wrong, a shared memory, and even a shared mythology. And for most midsize or larger organizations, HR is their temple. Managers are its local ministers. And HR professionals—or HRians, as I affectionately call us—are the temple priests and priestesses. HRians author the instructive hymnals and generously dispense them for employees to sing-song along. HRians are the organization's storytellers and historical archivists as well as its most zealous and adoring *amen corner*.

So, why am I telling you this? For many employees, human resources, HR, or personnel is a shadowy and enigmatic space, with a thick and impenetrable culture of secrecy and tentacles woven throughout the organization. Most know it is HR you call about sick days or 401(k)s. And most know HR will be calling you if they find you on the wrong side of policy. But what many don't see is the elaborate system of philosophy, practice, and process that results in some employees easily crossing over into leadership while others don't, despite really wanting to. These employees are among those who believe promoting into leadership is just a matter of strong performance or being on their boss' good side (or just not getting on their boss' bad side). They are mistaken. If only it were that simple. Still, let me be very clear: the relationship you have with your manager is of the utmost importance if you intend to climb. Their local influence, coaching, and advocacy of you and your ability are critical. But the power to move your career doesn't begin or end with them. Of all of the power managers in midsize and larger organizations can wield, the truth is, they take their agency and cues from somewhere else—HR.

Much like missionaries, HRians spread the principles and philosophies considered by that organization as the indisputable gospel. These "truths" are the organization's system of good and bad, what it considers strengths and flaws, and what is expected and accepted among the organization's righteous citizenry, especially among those it will call to lead. HR evangelizes about what exemplifies the exceptional, who are, in turn, blessed with more authority, more responsibility, more money, and more influence and are called leaders. HR, in alignment with the business units, elevates and promotes the people who are considered extraordinary and beautiful exemplars of whatever the organization values. At certain levels of the organization, these beautiful ones may even be regarded as untouchable, sacred cows, or in a political sense, even divine. Indeed, *they* giveth these gifts and *they* taketh away. And who, specifically, are *they*? They are HRians like HR Business Partners, talent management consultants, executive development folks, training and development professionals, and recruiting agents, as well as hiring managers along with other hierarchies of leadership in the business unit. The *theys* are all the organizational bodies that decide what leadership is, what it looks like, who has it, and who doesn't.

More Than the Stars Need to Align

I'm no heretic when I describe HR as a kind of church; I'm a true believer. I've been an HRian my entire professional life, and HR is where I learned the craft of helping people become who they could and would be. But as you pursue the next level of your leadership career, you should know the truth. And among the first things to understand is this: when you are looking at being elevated to the next level—especially if that means moving into a management position—look first for alignments. Like the stars align to form the celestial gods and goddesses of mythology, you must align and find connectivity within the constellation of your organization's systems, culture, and philosophy.

Finding this alignment may prove challenging. As with any ideology, what HR and the organization prize most may or may not line up with your particular priorities, logic, what you deem as reasonable or fair, or your personal values. You look in the mirror and see someone who is ready to lead or lead more extensively. But the organization looks at and measures the individuals it will promote against the most fundamental of motivations: surviving and thriving. Take a marker and highlight that: the organization's first, last, and most basic drive is self-preservation. Surviving and thriving are your organization's alpha and omega. Who you are and what you want has little to do with it.

An organization's leaders and managers are the most direct way a company advances these most basic objectives. An organization's leaders are its standard-bearers and culture carriers. Leaders adopt, model, and push the organization's culture down into the departments, where the employees live and breathe. Therefore, the organization recognizing you as leadership material is not so much for your benefit—although, for the leader, there are many benefits to be had—as it is the organization materializing what it needs for its own well-being. There is nothing wrong or diabolical in that. That's just smart business. Equally smart is looking for people who are willing and able to carry the organization's values into the departments and work teams with vigor and enthusiasm, where those values can be infused into coaching, business directives, and the messaging employees hear and work by.

If you are going to be a leader in a given organization, it is essential that your values and its values align; after all, you, as a leader, will be heavily leveraged to inspire employees' attachment to the organization's culture and adherence to its norms. Organizational values include the words or phrases that underpin its philosophy, code of behavior, and the essentials of its success. Values serve as the organization's conscience and compass as it navigates its way through change, risks, opportunity, and decision-making. They are part of the organization's self-perceived identity and, ideally, the pillars of its culture. And as one of the organization's leaders, your job will include keeping those pillars strong, upright, and polished.

An Insider Tip
Actions Are Louder Than Words

The first place you can look to find your organization's values is on its website. You'll likely see that your organization has gone through great effort to design a mission statement (the organization's reason for being) or a values statement (the beliefs that form the organization's identity and decision-making compass) that attempt to describe in words or phrases what it, as an entity, believes and stands for to prospective customers and partners. Organizations have come to understand that in today's marketplace, consumers have several choices that all offer nearly the same products and services. So what are the real differentiators that separate one business from another? What deems a company worthy or unworthy of its consumers' hard-earned dollars? The answer often is the organization's personality, culture, or what it espouses are its values.

But I encourage you to go a step further. Some organizations do not have explicitly described values. And then there are other organizations that have a statement, but it doesn't accurately describe what's valued in the organization on the ground, day to day. For that, look to your experiences as an employee, and ask yourself the following:

1. *What gets measured on performance reviews? What in the organization has a goal attached? (If the organization measures it, it matters.)*

2. *What behaviors get rewarded? What gets high praise? (This is what the organization wants repeated.)*

3. *What behaviors get punished or are actively discouraged? (The opposite of these will point to what it values.)*

4. *What do most managers and leaders in the organization have in common? (That shared attribute has worth attached to it.)*

If your company does not have a list of values, or if you suspect its espoused values do not match how it operates in reality, how you answer these questions can point to what you need to be or do to succeed in that environment.

My Confession

I am a seasoned HRian. I've been there when leadership job descriptions were conceived, drafted, and posted (or not posted, but nonetheless mysteriously filled). I've designed recognition programs and determined what leadership walk and talk we, as an organization, wanted repeated through reward and reinforcement. I've consulted in the discussions on who was considered a high-potential employee, that is, worthy of the investment of expensive and intensive leadership grooming. I confess I've been right there when we weighed who was the best choice for promotion. I knew who the *theys* chose and why. I knew who was not selected and why not. And I even knew the employees who would give their eyeteeth to be tapped on the shoulder for a plum role, and why they never would be.

Through the course of doing this work in HR, I've seen firsthand what organizations want in their leaders and by what yardsticks they elevate certain people to the next level. Some of what the *theys* want is explicit and plain to see. It's discussed in meetings. It's written on large placards in the corridors and taught in training classes. But just between you, me, and the lamppost, a lot of it isn't. A lot of it is quiet, subtle, and nuanced. And if there is anything HRians are good at, it is keeping things quiet, subtle, and nuanced. Much of an HRian's secrecy is justified. Human resources, after all, holds your most delicate pieces of information, your personal pedigree, your medical information, and other things that are no one else's beeswax but yours. Despite HR's legendary silence, some employees are lucky enough to have a mentoring manager, a coach, or a sponsor who can help them decode the company's expectations, which is essential to navigating their way to promotion. And the rest? They often get left behind and in the dark as to why no one can see them as leaders.

The Writing on the Wall

For many organizations, a serious threat is looming on the horizon these days. And on some issues, it's time for HRians like me to break our silence. According to organizational futurists, the Bureau of Labor Statistics, and other talent forecasts, there is a dire shortage of strong and suitable leadership candidates. That's not hyperbole; it means exactly what it says. As current leaders age and retire, many businesses are not confident in the quality or sustainability of their current leadership pipelines. That means when organizations look down the line at the next person who will occupy a leadership seat, as well as the person who will follow her, and the next person who will succeed him, and so on, the *theys* worry about the leadership readiness and capability they see and don't see. Remember, among an organization's core imperatives is surviving and thriving. But a thinning pool of potential leaders to deliver on those most basic objectives can quickly translate into a long, slow, and painful death. It's the kind of stuff that keeps executives up at night, and for good reason.

As formidable competitors multiply like rabbits in a volatile marketplace, a company's only true secret weapon is the quality of its leadership bench. But building that bench with ready and able leaders is daunting work. Compounding the problem is the rapid speed of change, the migration to automated and tech-driven jobs, and the need for agile workers that can go with the flow. Add to that the major shift in the available generations in the workplace, and with it, a shift in what will attract and keep good employees in their seats. Where will organizations find these desperately needed leaders? Should they *buy* them—as in recruiting the talent? Or should they *build* them—as in growing and developing the leadership skills in the people they already have? The *war for talent*, a term first coined by Steven Hankin of McKinsey & Company, is very real in its description of a marketplace that is full of organizations that are keen to buy, poach, clone, kidnap, grab, or steal leadership talent—and by any means necessary.[1]

Currently, even as I write this book, there are more jobs than there are workers to fill them. So why would an organization be so anxious when they have a sea of people to choose from? The abundance of talent only exists in the most general sense. When it comes to leadership, organizations engaged in the talent war need more than just warm butts in seats to stay competitive. They want and need the best their total rewards and compensation packages can attract. For leadership candidates coming to the table with the right stuff, the opportunities can be endless—and that makes having the right stuff, if you're a person who wants to rise, even more important.

In HR, none of this is news, but like everyone else, HRians can be slow to change. Secrecy continues to be a standard feature in the cultures of many HR departments. With some things, that's appropriate, but with other things, it's not. It's just not! HR and our internal clients, the business units, spend lots of time and mental energy cooking up lists of desirable behaviors and skills wanted in a good leader, and then we keep it secret. High-potential employees are identified in elaborate cross-functional talent review meetings, but that's often a secret too, even to the people who are on the list as the high potentials. In many organizations, employee development is a competency with which managers notoriously struggle. Managers are told to coach their people, but coaching is misunderstood as a one-sided lecture with punitive undertones. The *theys*, of which I was one, are good at telling employees what we don't want while never quite saying what we do want, or least not in ways that are clear, helpful, and pragmatically reflective of real organizational life.

If we in HR tell people what it really takes to be perceived and valued as promotable leadership material, I believe more people will rise to the challenge. So why we, in HR, have been so secretive about the mysterious calculus that produces ready-to-perform leaders makes little sense to me. That's why I've gone rogue and am spilling the beans. Although they are likely to revoke my HRian card, over the next several chapters, I'm about to sing like a canary about leadership as it is defined by organizations, what the *theys* want to see in a leader, and what you need to do to be recognized as one too. Although phrases alluding to a leadership shortage might seem scary, they suggest the opportunities to lead will be increasingly available to those who ready themselves. My deep belief is that if people understood that there's no magic to it, only an opportunity, the right knowledge, and informed choices, more people would endeavor to show up as the leaders they really are.

Getting Started

Your organization wants leaders cut from its cultural cloth because they will carry the organization's banner and lead its cultural chorus. While you are likely well acquainted with your organization, to get started, you need to refamiliarize yourself with it through a new lens: as an environment in which you will lead. Ask: What's important to your organization? What's its mission? What's its vision? What are its values, and do your values align? You want to be a leader, and let's say you get your wish. Congrats! But once the glow of recognition and promotion wears off, your chief task will be actualizing, with and through others, whatever is essential to your organization's survival and growth. Are you prepared to do that? Are you, in fact, cut from your organization's cloth?

Strategic Reflection No. 2

List five of your values. What are those universal truths you believe and use to navigate through life? Next, list five of your organization's values or business priorities. Compare the lists, and notice where they align and where they do not. What do you see most: alignment or division? Knowing that an organization actualizes its priorities through its leaders, how ready are you to be the standard-bearer of your organization's values? How comfortable are you, while embodying your own philosophies, in evangelizing those of your organization?

Your Values	Your Organization's Values
1.	1.
2.	2.
3.	3.
4.	4.
5.	5.

If your values don't align with those of the organization, now is the time to be honest—especially with yourself. Determine if this gap between values can be filled by you learning more about the organization's position. Or perhaps there is no amount of information that can reconcile your principles and those of your workplace. If it, unfortunately, is the latter, the question becomes, Why do you want to lead there? Luckily, at this early stage, there is only one wrong move you can make: focusing on the promotion and title (with its financial, social, and emotional perks) while ignoring an organizational culture you, in truth, find an itchy and ill-fitting coat to wear. You must discover elements within your organization's values with which you can authentically align. You will become a carrier of its culture. To do that well, you have to find yourself reflected in it, and it, in you.

Chapter 2

WHY THEY DON'T SEE LEADERSHIP IN YOU

Hard questions and the first of many answers

WHY DON'T THEY see leadership in you? That's the central question we need to answer. In this question, I can hear sadness. I can hear rejection, the seeds of insecurity, and a longing for an explanation. In this question, I can hear several others. It's a question with many layers. Let's decode the first few here and now.

The central question is bursting with many critical themes you will need to explore, starting with, why don't they see *leadership*? More to the point, what *is* leadership? And how do organizations and HR departments define it? What companies want in a leader can be frustratingly mysterious, especially when those who say you don't have *it* are also the ones who cannot tell you what *it* is.

Why don't *they see?* Also rising out of the question is the theme of the decision-making *theys* to whom you need to prove your readiness to step up. This theme is also about what is concealing your leadership qualities from the *theys'* line-of-sight. What tools, road maps, and secret knowledge do you lack that keeps your leadership unrealized, masked, or invisible?

And then there's: Why don't they see leadership *in you?* Of all of the themes, the most painful is embedded here too. It is a practical question as well as a rhetorical lament laced with increasing self-doubt: Why don't they see *you* as a leader? Why is this happening *to you?* Why is this not happening *for you?* Why *not you? Why?*

Suspended Animation

I found this central question, swollen with the themes buried within it, so intriguing that I built a whole book around it. One reason was the question's universality. Asking it were individual contributors who wanted to graduate into people management roles, as well as managers who wanted to be seen as high potentials on a fast track to more senior positions. Then there were some who were not particularly interested in managing teams at all. They wanted to be respected as subject-matter experts, internal consultants, or thought leaders in their companies, and they too, were asking this same awful, vexing, and crazy-making question. I became curious and interested in the circumstances of my clients and others in this situation. From what career infirmity did these people suffer? What was going on among those whose leadership was so masked, their future promotability was uncertain? What I found surprised me:

The central question occurred at all ranks and levels of hierarchy. Although the people I observed were at different levels in their organizations—salaried, hourly, managing people or managing processes and projects—those things didn't seem to matter a bit. Yes, a senior vice president is very different from a first-time team supervisor, but in the marrow, leadership is leadership is leadership. And no matter the hierarchical levels of the leaders I studied, I found that leadership in hiding—leadership the *theys* couldn't see—was perceived as leadership in absence. It didn't matter how much leadership capability or experience the individual may or may not have actually had. If the *theys* couldn't see it, it was perceived as not there. No level or hierarchical standing was immune. The invisibility of leadership, I found, could, and did, happen to anyone.

Experiencing the central question was easy. In fact, it was effortless. There were no dramatic crimes for which people were being punished and thus denied an upward trajectory in their organizations. Nonetheless, people desirous of upward growth—but denied—felt invisible, frustrated, even frozen by forces they did not understand. There were no embarrassing backstories, yet being seen as a bona fide leader still eluded them.

Naming the central question was hard. Some of the people I studied were very clear and direct about the source of their frustration, but most were not. Most could not specifically articulate their problem other than to say they were stuck. For most, it was the nuances in their stories that gave light to their problem. It was in these stories of stuckness that I first noticed what appeared to be categories of careers in suspended animation. After listening to hundreds of stories over the years, I cataloged nine distinct states of careers caught in paralysis, nine conditions that effectively froze promotability in place and masked the person's intention, ability, or potential to lead.

The Nine

Overpass'd

You went for it—the senior management role—just as you've done before, thinking surely this time would be different. Then they gave it to someone else with qualifications equal to your own. And if that wasn't painful enough, this marks the third time you've been passed over... and over... and over.

In Time Out

You said the words: "I want to be developed..." You asked because you are ready to take the reins to advance your career. You'll take whatever tools and training your boss will offer. What's not clear is whether your boss is taking you seriously, but what *is* clear, by the fact that nothing's happened, is that your boss is taking his own sweet time.

Battlefield Promotion

They threw you into a leadership role during a crisis. It was hard-fought, bloody, and took a lot of work, but you got things back on track and back to normal. But although you've not changed a thing, *now* they have concerns? *Now* they're unsure if you can lead?

Hamster Wheel

You want a management role. But you're not going to get it without experience. That's why you need the management role, which you can't get without the experience. How are you supposed to get experience without a management role, which would give you experience for the management role you want?

Stuck on Assistant

You're already in management—well, sort of. You're an assistant supervisor, an invisible and meaningless title, with no real authority unless the boss is on vacation. And even then, when it comes to their questions or concerns, the staff members say they'll just wait 'til the boss is back. Getting your manager and others to see you as a full-fledged leader seems so out of reach— 'cause all they see when they look at you is the assistant, the right-hand, the second in command—never the one in charge.

Fallen Star

Before this, all you had to worry about was playing your best game. So that's what you did, and that's why your bosses bumped you up into management. Now you're in the penalty box for not doing your job? Being the star player got you in the arena. So why does it seem that to stay in the spotlight, you will have to be something other than what put you there?

Out of Sight

You've kept your head down, your nose to the grindstone, pumping out good work, because sooner or later, someone's got to take notice. You've built the right skills, got the right experience, and displayed it all beautifully on the right résumé. It's everything that should help your leadership qualities stand out, loud and proud, except for the fact that no one's looking.

Untitled

They have all sorts of names for what you are: workhorse, worker bee, B player. But although all of them sound so commendable, what you really are is a seasoned specialist with a lot of experience and deep insight into what you do. You want them to see you as a specialized knowledge expert and thought leader—not just a solid performer, but their trusted, go-to person.

Golden Cage

Besides being really good at what you do, you're a rare bird with a unique and high-value set of skills. But when it's time to fly to the next level, they clip your wings. They want you where you are, laying your golden eggs. Leaving the company? Not an option; you have a lot invested. But there's no getting over the irony: what they most respect and reward in you is the very thing keeping you caged.

Strategic Reflection No. 3

In what ways is your career in suspended animation? Which categories reflect elements of your career stuckness? Which of the Nine most resonated with you?

_____

_____

_____

_____

_____

_____

Although I gave the Nine situationally descriptive "names" to enable our discussion about one versus the other, each of these scenarios is based on actual experiences of real people. Every. Single. One. I have witnessed or consulted on each in my coaching practice, and not just once. I've heard them repeatedly from a variety of people, with little variation. No wonder people become discouraged. And it doesn't stop there. People whose careers are in suspended animation often disengage from their teams or companies. Their enthusiasm is replaced by frustration, and sooner or later, that frustration turns in on itself, showing up as a decline in their quality of work or as an aggrieved attitude. They begin to doubt themselves and what they can achieve as they watch others climb into the roles they want and could perform with the right support. Otherwise talented people get talked out of—or worse, talk *themselves* out of—something that would be well within the realm of their possibilities if they only understood the situation for what it *really* is.

An Insider Tip
You Can't Be What You Can't See

Twentieth-century sociologist Robert Merton, who coined the term self-fulfilling prophecy, theorized that whatever we believe about a circumstance, we will help manifest. How? We will operate in ways that confirm our expectations. What ever we see or believe of ourselves, we will prove right through our actions or by cherry-picking the affirmative points in the available data. Also known as confirmation bias, the behavior describes our likelihood to confirm, seek alignment with, cause, or bring to fruition the outcome we always expected to see. [2]

Can you see yourself as a leader?

The next time you consider or apply for a next-level role, first picture yourself in the position. The how, ways, and means are not important right now. Right now, just see yourself making the decisions, solving the problems, and influencing the people around you. Picture yourself handling a day when things go well. See yourself handling a day when things go poorly.

If the movie in your mind comes easily, press play and repeat. You will need that image as motivation as you traverse the path toward what you want. Expect the picture to sharpen and change as you acquire the skills, knowledge, and confidence to build your career success story. And over time, with belief, choice, work—and an opportunity, you will begin to see evidence of its veracity and of its becoming. But if you cannot see yourself in a next-level role, here too, you will prove yourself correct. If the picture in your head remains blurry and out of focus, examine potential reasons. Ask yourself what you really believe about your capacity to become a leader. Do you see yourself as having the raw materials for it? Examine what thoughts and beliefs would help the picture crystalize in your mind's eye—because if you cannot see yourself climbing to what's next at work, can you really expect others to?

Clarity, at Last

So let's end this chapter where we began, with the most vexing question of all: Why don't they see leadership in you? The answer is this: of all the admirable things there are to see in you, your invisibility as a leader rises out of the three things the *theys* don't see:

1. your evident and discernible value-add;

2. your scaled responsiveness to a variety of situations; and

3. a unique, intentional, and compelling association between you and positive outcomes, better known as your leadership brand.

Put a different way, the *theys* can't see the value you bring to the work. The way you respond doesn't match the size or scale of the situations in which you are expected to lead, and your leadership value isn't delivered in a way that is consistent, reliable, and known as uniquely yours. All other things being equal, these are the reasons people at work aren't putting leadership and you in the same sentence.

What is evident and discernible value? What does it mean to be responsive to the size and scale of a particular circumstance? And how do you make all that uniquely yours? Let's go deeper; there are more answers just ahead.

Chapter 3

THE WHITE RABBIT

What and why leadership is

WHY ALL THE fuss about leadership? Why do we want it? Why do we want people to see us as worthy of following? Why is the prospect of it so seductive while the mastery of it, for most, remains allusive? I've often thought of leadership as the White Rabbit in Lewis Carroll's *Alice's Adventures in Wonderland*.[3] Like the well-dressed hare, a central character of the story, leadership is hard to pin down and hard to define, but we chase it. We can't help it; leadership is irresistible. For millennia, we have had the impulse to pursue it, with the hope of unlocking what it is. But lucky for us, there are breadcrumbs—small clues we can piece together— just by looking at leadership's interesting life story.

Leadership—the Quick-and-Dirty Version

Around 380 BC, Plato was among the first notable Western philosophers to write extensively on the subject of leadership in his Socratic dialogue *The Republic.*[4] For the purposes of our conversation, four key lessons rise out of his work:

1. Leadership is an important but mysterious body of work, so we come by our curiosity honestly. We know it when we see it and feel its impact, but even the world's best thinkers have continuously struggled to know of what it's made.

2. Leadership is about the leader in relationship to others. There is no leadership in isolation. Leadership happens through, with, for, and because of others.

3. Leadership is about influencing action in others to achieve something of virtue, of value, or to achieve a changed and improved state. Process is important too, but leadership focuses on purpose. It's not a mechanical exercise; it's about the mission. It is not a transactional unit of work; leadership is about a trans-formed and better result.

4. Leadership is driven not by just one strength, attri-bute, or trait but through a collection, working together to cause a specific outcome.

Despite Plato's thorough analysis, what leadership is would continue to be vigorously debated well into the 1900s. Quite a can of worms he opened there.

Fast-forward about 2,200 years. (I said quick and dirty, didn't I?) In the 1800s, we see Thomas Carlyle, a Scottish philosopher and writer, push the great man and hero theories, which claimed leadership was a matter of birth, not learning.[5] Infant onesies and sippy cups notwithstanding, these theories said that only some individuals were born with magical leadership genes. But later, a newer theory conceded that it wasn't magic genes; it was dramatic *scenes*. English philosopher and biologist Herbert Spencer advanced that leadership didn't reside in the DNA. Rather, ordinary people were made extraordinary by the scenery and backdrop of intense circumstance—calamity, war, or zombie apocalypse. Amid the wind and fire of disaster, revolution, or the undead, the leader was forged.[6] So it wasn't a magical birth after all that made leaders but a cataclysmic accident of happenstance or, as American mythologist and sociologist Joseph Campbell coined it, a hero's journey.[7]

About one hundred years or so later, a different theory prevailed. English statistician Francis Galton argued the notion that leaders have a collection of traits deficient in nonleaders.[8] Beneficially, this theory contributed to the rise of leadership testing, assessment, and analysis as social scientists tried to understand the precise trail mix of leadership traits, granola, dried fruit, and nuts to constitute the perfect recipe. But it was that pesky word *traits* that proved problematic. As a brown-eyed girl, the windows to my soul are the result of genetic traits, making trait theory little more than a redux of the great man theory.[9]

By the 1940s, the seminal research of Kurt Lewin, Ronald Lippitt, and Ralph White asserted that leadership was behavioral.[10] Leaders simply *did* things nonleaders didn't do. In the 1960s, seeded by Spencer's work and later advanced by psychologist Paul Hersey and author Ken Blanchard, leadership was understood to be situational.[11] A leader couldn't be a one-trick pony. A behavior well suited in one situation might not be at all helpful in the next. Leaders had to be responsive to the circumstances they were in. During the 1970s, through the work of consultant Peter Drucker, historian James MacGregor Burns and then, later, professors John Kotter and Warren Bennis, we saw a groovy set of theories that clearly differentiated management—the tactics of aligning people and tasks, from leadership—the craft of moving others toward a beneficial outcome.[12, 13, 14, 15] As a result of that distinction, management theory *boogied on over* into its own separate and parallel universe.

And then came a new twist—a term thought to have been first coined in 1997 by business consultant Tom Peters: self-packaging or #LeadershipBrand. In the age of selfies and social media, brand reputation is no longer just the domain of things that are bought and sold. Brand reputation is also relevant to you and the value others associate with your leadership ability. Further, it must be a value you provide purposefully versus—*oops!*—by accident. Your brand, or the value the *theys* associate with you, directly drives followership and other people's willingness to be influenced and aligned with your plan of action.[16]

Based on our brisk walk with the ghost of leadership's past, what is significant to take away is that defining leadership has always been tricky; so go easy on the *theys* when they struggle to say what they want from you. Leadership is about influencing a valuable and transformational outcome. Leadership success depends on your responsiveness to the situation and context, and it all works together to create and influence your reputation, or leadership brand. Fueled by choice and intention, leadership is the product of many things you choose to do that nonleaders do not. That's the good news. Leadership is not genetic. We all have a shot; you only have to choose it. And that's also the bad news: You must *choose* it. There are particular things you must choose to do within the right context and on purpose to be a leader in ways people can see, feel, and appreciate.

Strategic Reflection No. 4

How would you describe leadership? List at least ten attributes. When you look at your defining list, circle and contrast the characteristics that are matters of behavior and choice versus those that reflect accidents of birth.

1.

2.

3.

4.

5.

6.

7.

8.

9.

10.

Leadership: Why We Love to Love You

Although we will all define it in our own terms, the evolving study of leadership tells us definitively why we pursue it: because leadership causes a valuable change. And why is that important? Because my mama said so! Although I was just an ankle biter in OshKosh B'gosh jeans, I vividly remember the theme on which my mother, an elementary school teacher, waxed poetic every year. For me, the daffodils did not herald spring. Instead, it was my mother rehearsing her life-cycles lecture, which climaxed with the phrase, "All living things grow and change. All living things must grow and change, or they die." And then there's evolutionary scientist Charles Darwin, whose work argued that it wasn't the strongest or the smartest of a species that survives. It's the ones who can adapt; it's the ones who can change.[17] Mom and Mr. Darwin cinched it for me: change is the engine of life.

There's something intuitive about it, this inexorable relationship between change and life. I think we love and chase leadership because through it, there is positive change, which is critical to a system surviving and thriving. All living systems—a body, a people, a family, a team, an organization—must change to survive. That's what leaders do: they facilitate positive change. Change is going to happen regardless. We exist in a river of steadily rushing water. Although you stand still, everything around you is in a state of perpetual movement, a state of change. Leadership helps us move along with that fluidity or counter to it in a preferred direction. Through leaders, we can keep pace with the velocity, ride the water, and even harness its power and momentum.

Let's look at four people who are causing positive change in their organizations in different ways and at different hierarchical levels. Meet our case study subjects: Petra, Trey, Jacob, and Kat.

Case Study: Petra

Petra is a director of market development leading a sizable team of supervisors and individual contributors. She and her team recently caused positive change by creating a presence in a previously untapped market in the city. The new revenue stream, the newly situated company sites, and the new jobs therein meant a shared win between the company and the community.

Case Study: Trey

Trey is a senior project manager and subject-matter expert (SME) in information technology (IT). He handles many complex systems and processes in his division. Although Trey does not manage people, he frequently stands in the role of project leader for a cross-functional team of peers and partners. Recently, Trey caused a valuable and positive change by upgrading a long-standing but flawed system in the department. Though centralized at the home office, IT includes widely dispersed sub-teams across the organization's footprint. Without the upgrade, the various parts of IT would be unable to communicate effectively. A breakdown in that network would have dire impacts to the complex systems that support the organization's operations. So although seemingly a singular and localized issue, Trey's work had enterprise-wide impacts.

Case Study: Jacob

Jacob is a senior client specialist and an individual contributor. He works in customer service and recently caused positive change by helping a senior citizen and longstanding customer navigate the new design of her confusing account statement. More than a nice gesture, it went a long way in calming her initial distress, retaining her business, and ultimately, helping other employees who were dealing with similar customer complaints.

Case Study: Kat

Kat is an analyst in finance. She works within a large team of people who collectively generate financial analytics for other lines of business within the organization. She doesn't manage anyone, nor does she have any direct external customers. Kat, her manager, and her coworkers bring together different pieces of data to generate high-demand and high-complexity reports. Like links in a chain, every person's work feeds the next. The team's success depends on its ability to convert cooperation and communication into an open channel through which the work can flow smoothly and quickly. A breakdown between two or more people can cause choke points that can delay vital information that drives essential deci-sion-making across the enterprise. Although it's been a lengthy and sometimes uncomfortable process, the positive change Kat made was within herself. She had to concentrate her sharp wits on managing her sharp tongue, which, according to feedback her boss conveyed, had resulted in unexpected and negative impacts to the flow of work the team was responsible for producing. Kat had to work at it daily, but her ability to manage her communication style, her work relationships, as well as her emotional intelligence grew stron-ger by the day.

Each of these employees is engaged in change. For some it is substantial; for others, the change is small. But are they all leaders? Are they all promotable? That we will discover as we go. But remember this: what differentiates leadership from other social phenomena is its unique ability to facilitate change. And not just any change. Leaders create change that is helpful. They cause change that adds value. Arguably, two things motivate human beings: avoiding pain and accelerating contact with an advantage. It's true of the individual, the group, the department, and the organization. Leaders cause change that adds value, and that value, to some degree, in big ways or small, helps the organization avoid a threat or bring on an advantage. This, friends, is the core purpose of leadership: to cause change that adds value.

Strategic Reflection No. 5

What positive change happens because of you or the work you perform? How do you help your organization (its systems, its people, its products, or its customers) avoid a threat or accelerate contact with an advantage?

_____

_____

_____

_____

_____

An Insider Tip
Upgrade Your Introduction

When people meet someone new in the elevator, at a networking luncheon, or at a company mixer, shortly after the exchange of names, the question, "So what do you do?" inevitably comes up. Most people smile and answer that question with their job title. But that's a missed opportunity.

Unless that person works in the cubicle next to you, most organizational job titles are descriptively meaningless except to the person who has it, the organizational chart, and the HRians who gave the role that name for the benefit of the HR database. It does nothing to describe how you add value. When I meet someone new at a networking event and say, "Hi, I'm Damaris. I'm a coach and consultant," in the best-case scenario, the puzzled person in front of me is thinking, Hmmm, what's that? Which is quickly followed up by, Whatever. And, Where's the bar?

Why? Because my title isn't relevant to others, only the value I add is. So I may do better if I say, "I'm Damaris. I help people become more promotable to next-level positions at work." This small adjustment immediately boosts clarity so that others don't have to work very hard to understand what I do, or more importantly, how I add value.

Getting Started

Wanting to be a leader is a good and worthy aspiration. Give yourself permission to want what you want, especially now that you know what is at the core of it: causing positive change and value. The problem is, *wanting* isn't the same as *getting*. To raise your promotability and the *theys'* perception of you as leadership material, you must do more than *want*.

You can start by getting clear on two fundamentals. First, you should be able to identify what change occurs when you successfully execute your job. However, answering that only gets you halfway there. If I move my office wastepaper basket from here to across the room, yes, a change has occurred, but unless I'm practicing my trashcan free throws, it is not a significant one. Change has to be connected to value. Leaders don't just cause change; leaders cause change *and* value. Something of significance should improve, diminish, increase, decrease, be dismantled, or be built up as a result of the change you facilitate.

You should be able to identify how the change you cause benefits or creates advantages for the organization, the group, the customers, or the bottom line. Or perhaps the change you cause helps the organization dodge a threat or disadvantage. All your arguments, business cases, résumés, interviews, or pitches regarding your leadership potential and promotability should rise from your ability to articulate the change you cause and the value that change creates. But even if you learn to recognize your impact and value, it doesn't mean others will. And the twin trouble keeping your leadership value under lock and key may be to blame.

Chapter 4

LEADERSHIP IS AS LEADERSHIP DOES

What's keeping your leadership capability hidden in plain sight

IT'S TIME YOU faced the facts: you will never, ever arrive at leadership. That's because it's not a place. It's not a noun—not in the practical sense anyway. It's a verb, an action word. Leadership moves, and it has an impact as a result of moving. But even that knowledge is not enough to realize your goal. *Seeing is believing*; when the *theys* don't believe what they see in you is indicative of a leader, arrival is a moot point. If your leadership is hidden, if your career is stuck in suspended animation, a pair of troublesome twins is the likely culprit. The laments of the Nine echo in this double threat to your promotability. Highly effective at masking the leader you really are, these two leadership frailties can kill your opportunities to excel and ascend at work.

Doing Leadership

You have likely heard the saying, "If it waddles like a duck, quacks like a duck, looks like a duck, it's a duck." And how do we know? Because the short, feathered creature looks like, moves like, and sounds like a duck. It's *doing* itself as a duck does. It carries its nature on its face. So does leadership. We know it because of the way it behaves. For some, one lock on your leadership may be about you not knowing how to *do* leadership, especially in ways the *theys* can recognize. The doing or the behaviors indicative of leaders in most organizations are what HRians refer to as leadership competencies.

You see, it's all about the birds. When we think about how a pterodactyl behaves versus a duck, for example, it becomes evident that the doing or the manifestation of a thing is not expressed in a single action or feature. Feathers alone don't make it a duck. The bill alone doesn't make it a duck. The gait and movements alone don't make it a duck. It's all those things working together that create an outcome indicative of the cute waterfowl we know and love. It's all those things working together that create the result that, despite some similarities, allows us never to confuse it with the giant winged predators of the Jurassic period. The same can be said of leadership competencies. Competencies are the positive and valuable result of several intentional behaviors, skills, and characteristics working together to accomplish an expected and desirable outcome.

An Insider Tip
If You Want It, Know What It Looks Like

You would never go to a job interview without researching the company first. Don't pursue a leadership position or promotion without investigating what competencies are expected of you either. Most organizations identify what competencies they believe will best drive their business priorities. These requirements can also be called standards or can be articulated as parts of a leadership framework. Whatever your organization calls them, find out what they are. Use the following questions as a guide:

1. *What business outcome is this leadership role responsible for achieving?*

2. *What leadership competencies are believed to drive that outcome in this role?*

3. *How does this organization define these competencies?*

4. *How does the absence of these competencies leave the organization vulnerable or weakened?*

Use the answers to organize data points on your résumé, to strategize an upcoming interview, or to build a development plan around any of the desired competencies that, at this point, you may lack.

Understanding leadership competencies is that simple, yet not simple at all. Let's revisit one of our case studies.

Case Study: Kat, Finance Analyst

One of the reasons Kat's manager was keen to give feedback on the negative impact his employee was having on others was an episode he, himself, had experienced with Kat's infamous manner. There was a seat open on a highly esteemed committee that engaged in plum assignments and high-visibility projects. The manager used the coveted seats as a reward and as stretch assignments for employees he wanted to develop because he saw them as having leadership potential. And when Kat learned she was not getting the open seat, the employee was downright indignant.

Kat marched into her boss' office with a list of qualities she had been told were desired in committee members, pointed to assertiveness, and explained how at this very moment she was demonstrating it, yet was still being denied the coveted seat. "Why?" she demanded to know. Kat's action of confronting her boss was arguably a demonstration of the word assertiveness. But when her manager pointed to other words and phrases listed as committee member requirements, like brainstorming, strong communication, problem solving, conflict resolution, and civility, a different picture emerged. Assertiveness alone would not convert into and cause the committee's primary objective and value-add: generating ideas via team brainstorming. That would require a committee member who could assert their unique voice compellingly, while also supporting and collaborating with others in what amounted to a strategic think tank. Yes, assertiveness was among the requirements. But there were also many other behaviors that, disappointingly, Kat was nowhere near demonstrating.

Many people who are trying to stand out as leadership material and promotable at work make a similar misstep. Did you spot it? Yes, Kat was rude, but her mistake goes deeper than that. Like Kat, some leadership contenders suffer from a kind of myopia or single vision. They latch on to one narrow descriptor, one qualification, or one requirement while ignoring the aggregate of the feathers, the bill, and the waddle that makes it a whole duck. What Kat forgot was that the *theys* look for people who cause change *and* value. The *theys* want someone who demonstrates the competency completely. Unfortunately for employees like Kat, in ignoring the competency in full, the ability to cause the intended value *in full* is also lost.

An Insider Tip
You'd Better Ask Somebody

If your company hasn't named the competencies it values, here are three ways to ferret them out:

1. *Ask someone. Your manager is a great place to start. The question is simple: "What leadership competencies or leadership behaviors does the organization or department value?" Ask which competencies or behaviors your manager specifically prioritizes. Another great source of information is in the human resources department, specifically the recruiter who hired you. You were credible enough for that person to help get you into a job. Leverage that relationship again. The recruiter would have the list of competencies and behaviors or at least a sense of what the organization or a particular department values and wants to see in the people occupying its leadership roles.*

2. *Research leadership competencies in general. Search "leadership competencies" and get ready to find a vast number of responses, but don't get overwhelmed. If you look closely, you will likely notice that the same competencies are used repeatedly, in different combinations, by a variety of industries. But you can expect that competencies gener-*

ally fall into the following three focus areas: self-management, relationship management/ influence, and strategy/business management. Based on what you know about your organization, think about what three competencies seem essential in each of those categories. Be observant and notice which competencies your company most consistently rewards, and you'll be looking at what the organization most values.

3. *Keep reading. There is a leadership framework or a collection of typically desirable leadership competencies, covering all three focus areas, just a few chapters away.*

Kat's not alone when it comes to misunderstanding what competencies are and how they are used to eliminate or include contenders for leadership opportunities. Few do. But I'm about to sneak you into the HRian's world of competencies, criteria, and efficient wordplay, after which you will never look at an internal job posting or interview quite the same way again.

Job Postings: Never as Much as *and* More Than Meets the Eye

I remember a discussion I had with a client a few years ago. She was lamenting rather dramatically about being passed over… again. At one point, she exclaimed, with theatrics on full throttle, "I met every single qualification on the posting. And none of it mattered. I didn't even get an interview!" I told her what few people outside of HR know: Although the job posting and job description are seemingly targeted to promotion seekers like her, they are, in fact and moreover, talent-selection tools and thus are really designed to serve recruiters and hiring managers.

Just look at a garden-variety job posting. It will include a title and a brief description of the role before it goes into a qualification-by-qualification list of what the job requires. But here's the truth of it: the first purpose of the job posting is to separate the *maybes* and the *mights* from the *shouldn'ts* and *never wills*. Job postings initially help would-be candidates self-select in or out of applying. Although you rarely need to meet every one, the lists of have-to-have and nice-to-have qualifications are there to help some people recognize that they do not possess enough of the requirements and thus opt out on their own. This saves recruiters and hiring managers the time and effort of weeding out the *can't-possiblys* and the *never-should-haves*.

When the *theys* search for the next person to promote into leadership, they use the checklist of qualifications for scarcely any other purpose than to narrow the field of prospects who should have disqualified themselves and didn't. This, in part, explains some of those mysterious postings to which you apply but never receive an interview. The *theys* may have disqualified candidates they think should have self-selected out on their own. Those employees didn't, so the *theys* did it for them. Other times, the *theys* already know who they want in the job, or *where* they want to search, which may be outside the organization for external talent. This weeding-out process makes way for the true test, which comes later.

Big Things in Small Packages

Although competencies can seem to be much ado about nothing, they actually serve many practical purposes, especially for the *theys*, who are gatekeeping the next-level opportunities you want. Therefore, you should know a bit about how and why they are used. As you plot your strategy around your success story at work, these small, subtle, and little-known aspects of career climbing, for those who know, can pay big dividends. And for those who don't, these same elements can present big and perplexing obstacles. One of the most important things you need to understand is that competencies are often the language the *theys* use to describe what they are looking for in candidates. In a given organization, the *theys* choose a unique collection of competencies they believe, when demonstrated by leadership, will nurture and advance business objectives. Remember, it is always about executing on the business' objectives.

Many behaviors create a single competency. Several competencies drive business imperatives and make leadership evident or something the *theys* can see. "Leads with authenticity," for example, is a competency many organizations want in their leaders. Authentic leaders relate to others openly and positively and, despite having formal or informal authority and power, demonstrate having a down-to-earth and honest understanding of their own strengths and limitations. Authentic leadership is valuable because it supports and accelerates trust. And what's the business value in that? A trusted leader can easily influence others to work toward a positive and strategic change.

Leads with authenticity. So much gets accomplished in those few words. There isn't just one thing at work inside the phrase *leads with authenticity*—there are many. One of these, for instance, is *humility*. To be authentic, a person has to have a modest, balanced, and realistic view of him- or herself. Another ingredient is *openness* or, for better or worse, being transparent and easy for others to know. Out of the words *humility* and *openness* (and others such as *accountability* and *consistency*), rises the competency of authenticity. Authenticity is just the outcome of all those behaviors coming together in a nice, neat little package. Authenticity isn't so much of a descriptor, then, as it is a result—a result that achieves a particular business outcome. Again, it comes down to business outcomes.

Even Too Much of a Good Thing Is Bad

There's a cryptic adage I like that says: "No one is ever just one thing." The line is highlighting that people are complex. We have sides to us—some good; some, perhaps, not so good. This is true of most things, including words, even the words you'd think would be good at describing how ready you are to lead. That brings me to another reason why competencies are important to understand, and you can find that reason in the most unexpected place: the north and south poles.

Let's look at the word *humility* by itself. For most, humility is seen as a positive, as in someone who is unpretentious and avoids the appearance of self-importance. But could something like humility ever be a bad thing? Absolutely. If humility was overused, for example, suddenly something most think of as a positive can become a negative, as in someone with a weakened sense of self and low confidence. Any behavior or characteristic under the sun can be used properly, or overused, or used in the wrong place, at the wrong time, with the wrong person. That behaviors can shine as well as cast a shadow is the law of polarity at work. It says that all things have a north pole *and* south pole. Nothing is ever just one thing. All things have two extremes. Things are good *and* evil, possess strengths *and* limitations, depending on the eye, interpretation, and circumstance of the beholder. If each behavior within a leadership competency is taken on its own, each one is subject to polarity: the benefits of the behavior when used well and the consequences of the behavior when it is not.

Strategic Reflection No. 6, Part 1

In the space provided, make a list of three personal characteristics you take pride in. For each of your characteristics, use a few words to describe its potentially positive and negative impacts. Here's my list as an example:

	Well Used	Poorly Used
1. Creative	I use unconventional ways to solve problems.	I can recreate or overengineer simple processes.
2. Ambitious	I have clear goals and aspirations for my future.	I can seem competitive and opportunistic.

3. Independent	I'm self-sufficient and self-directed.	I may appear resistant to teamwork.

Strategic Reflection No. 6, Part 2

Next, look at the characteristics you noted in the far-left column, not as separate elements but as different ingredients that are going into one pot and simmering together. Capturing all three characteristics, generate a resulting competency, as well as a brief description that highlights the behaviors' combined business value. For example:

	Well Used	**Poorly Used**
1. Creative	I use unconventional ways to solve problems.	I can recreate or overengineer simple processes.
2. Ambitious	I have clear goals and aspirations for my future.	I can seem competitive and opportunistic.
3. Independent	I'm self-sufficient and self-directed.	I can appear resistant to teamwork.

The outcome and business value: Entrepreneurial spirit—a self-driven and innovative business approach to change and problem solving		
	Well Used	**Poorly Used**
1.		
2.		
3.		
The outcome and business value:		

Again, every characteristic taken on its own can be broken down into its positives and negatives, its shiny and shadowy sides. When interviewing, avoid describing yourself using a list of individual characteristics or behaviors to illustrate your leadership readiness. As we have demonstrated, when you itemize your characteristics, you leave it to the interviewer's perspective to decide which pole is used to define each one. But that's not how competencies work. When we eat chocolate chip cookies, most don't think about the flour, or the eggs, or the baking soda separately—each of which would be fairly unappetizing on its own. When we eat chocolate chip cookies, we enjoy the outcome. We enjoy the end result. When it comes to your leadership capability, the same phenomenon applies. Each of your characteristics, when considered individually, may or may not be seen as a positive. But when they are combined, their positive end result is a competency—and that's mmm, mmm good. Remember, competencies are the positive outcome of many things working together. When interviewing, emphasize what that combined value is. Just as it says on a dollar bill: *e pluribus unum*, or "out of the many, one."

Then It Was Pithy; Now It's Proof

Imagine that you are looking at a job description. The requirements on our make believe job posting are listed as five or so pithy competencies. By using these few competency-laden lines, what the *theys* have done is simplify the complexity that a long list of itemized characteristics would have created. Let's further imagine that the five competencies on our imaginary job description are pregnant with—and are the result of twenty-five or more behaviors. The *theys* used these competencies as a kind of shorthand for efficiency's sake, not for yours. What you need to understand now is, in the interview, you cannot take the same efficient approach. In the interview, you cannot simply stand on a few competencies to make the case that you are ready to lead.

Although it is a competency desired by the organization, simply saying you are authentic, for example, will not paint a credible picture of your ability to actually be it. Saying you are authentic is nice, but it is subjective and just your opinion—and like belly buttons, everyone has one. It would be like saying there's a duck at your feet to someone who is not there to witness it. It's likely to come off as an unanchored statement and even a lil' delusional to someone who's not standing there with you and your little feathered friend. But when you can support your claim by explaining that the thing at your feet has a bill and waddles and is sporting feathers, you have made a stronger case that you are, in fact, for some inexplicable reason, in the company of a duck. Likewise, you cannot simply claim you are authentic. But you can discuss and give positive examples of you demonstrating the combination of accountability, openness, and humility. You can explain how the combined behaviors that make you authentic help you produce a helpful business result: trust. You can provide a complete image that the *theys* can picture and, in their mind's eye, observe. And what happens is that you, your pet duck, and your authenticity become way more credible.

Give the People What They Really Want

The truest test of your competency claim is not a list of pleasant-sounding words that are all subject to the interviewer's polar interpretation. Nor is it in your stated claim to be able to leap tall buildings or catch bullets in your teeth. The truest test of your competency claim is in your discussion of achieving the business results the competency in question is designed to yield. When it comes to the interview, your ability to cause business results is what you are there to prove. Although it won't be stated this way, here is what your interviewer really wants answered: *Do you possess the competency? And if so, what results have you leveraged with it? And if you achieved those results in a previous department or role, can you do it again, using those same competencies, in mine?*

So what would it sound like, you effectively describing your abilities in a way that balances the pole-neutralizing effects of speaking in the language of competencies, with being able to provide the details that make it more credible in the ear of the interviewer? Imagine you are telling the hiring manager about your ability to win over a new client. You could say, having read the requirements on the job description, "Yeah, my clients find me authentic," as if you are checking off a competency box. Or you could connect the desired competency, along with the business result it yields with a bridge of brief and descriptive details, sounding something like this: "Authenticity was critical to getting results in my last role. I worked hard to be open and real with my clients. I got to know them. And they got to know me. But I was still their agent, so I made myself accountable for every step in their buying experience, from start to finish. Yeah, authenticity, I think, is what sealed the deal." What you have done is focus on your outcomes, backed up by the credibility-building details in a way that mirrors the competency the *theys* are after.

An Insider Tip
Answer with Outcomes

Before your next interview, preplan the outcomes you will discuss as evidence of your readiness for the role you want.

1. *Make a list of characteristics that describe you. But just as you demonstrated in Strategic Reflection No. 6, each of those descriptors has a positive and negative side. Never answer an*

> *interviewer with just a list of characteristics about yourself. How each item you list is interpreted may be difficult to predict.*

2. *Look at your list and think about the positive outcome those characteristics, when combined, have produced for you. Think about the problems you have solved or the needs you have served when your characteristics work together.*

3. *When you answer interview questions, lead with the positive outcome your combined characteristics create. Then, secondarily, itemize the individual elements that bring that outcome to fruition.*

Everyone Loves a Good Story

Many recruiters use a technique called behavioral inter viewing. Based on the premise that the best evidence of future conduct is past conduct, in behavioral interviewing, the recruiter or hiring manager asks for examples, stories, and anecdotes that demonstrate your having used a particular capability. Some HRians believe that asking hypothetical questions that begin with, "What would you do if..." only tests an applicant's ability to think fast and generate a hypothetical answer on the fly. Although hypothetical questions answer what you *could do* or *might do*, behavioral interviewing questions discuss what you *did do, have done,* and will likely do again under similar conditions.

Behavioral interviewing questions begin with phrases such as, "Tell me about a time when you exhibited [fill in the blank]," typically followed with, "So in the end, what was the outcome?" Here, the recruiter is testing your possession of a particular competency by requesting a retelling of a past experience where you displayed the required behaviors. Proponents believe the answers this kind of interviewing yields are more credible because they demand an actual memory and, thus, expose better evidence of possessing and using a particular skill. Furthermore, behavioral interviewing focuses on the outcome: the ultimate value that was added. Behavioral interviewing's appeal is the notion that if you delivered value in a past role, you will be able to deliver it again in a future role.

Before your next interview, take what you understand about your organization's favorite competencies and prepare anecdotes highlighting how, in past roles, you have demonstrated the competencies the organization values. Remember to land on the positive outcome your abilities ultimately produced. Whether you experience a behavioral interview or not, having actual stories of times when you demonstrated the behaviors that drive the desired competency can't hurt your bid for a next-level position one bit. Even if your interviewer isn't using that method, at worst, you are capitalizing on the effectiveness of storytelling, which is compelling due to its immersive, emotion provoking, and relatability features. People like stories. People believe stories.

A leader must add value to an organization. In an interview for a next-level role, the *theys* want to hear about you delivering the value the competency yields, especially when you can back it up with examples, stories, or anecdotes of you exhibiting the skills that make the competencies come to life. Leadership competencies essentially describe how to *do leadership* within that particular organizational culture. When it comes to interviewing for next-level positions at work, your ability to *do leadership* is everything—well, almost.

Seeing Is Believing

Knowing how to *do* what your organization defines as leadership is one thing, but a major obstacle keeping you hidden remains: the optics, or the *theys* having a line of sight on the value you create in the organization. Visibility is more than you pantomiming your way through a set of behaviors in front of others as if you were doing the Electric Slide. There's a saying that goes, "Rocking chairs move, but they don't go anywhere." Visibility is about the *theys* witnessing not just you doing leadership or using your competencies but also—and arguably more so—others experiencing the positive movement your competencies create.

There's another saying I like: "It's not enough to be good. People have to see you being good." One of my favorites, this adage emphasizes the fact that leadership competency isn't enough; *the doing of leadership* is not enough. You must create a result, an outcome, and an impact, and it must be something the *theys* can see. Mind you, their seeing you add value doesn't need to be literal. Even hearing about the positive impact and drawing a straight line between it and the competencies you used to drive that outcome will suffice. If the *theys* don't know about the value your leadership provides, your leadership provides no value. And if it offers no value, it's not leadership. It's nothing at all.

The Terrible Two

"If a tree falls in the forest and no one's around to hear it, does it make a sound?" You have likely heard this question before. It's one of those eternally vexing and existential questions one contemplates, along with "Why *did* that chicken cross the road?" and whether it—had the egg, or the egg—had it. As for the tree and its dubious descent, I imagine it as powerful, impactful, and as serving a variety of functions. It provides cover, pumps oxygen into the environment, serves as a habitat for animals, and is a contributing part of a larger ecosystem. These things constitute the value the tree provides. How does the tree add that value? It stands tall, extends its branches, and grows leaves; engages in photosynthesis; grows fruits and nuts; and has cozy and hidden knots, pockets, nooks, and crannies. These might be considered the competencies of the tree. And for something to be a tree, it must *do* itself in a manner that is *tree-like*. Likewise, leaders are powerful, impactful, and serve a particular function. To be called a leader, you must *do* yourself in a manner that is *leader-like*. If you do not understand what your organization and the *theys* define as leader-like, it should be no surprise why the leader you really are is in the shadows.

Situating the tree in your mind's eye is only half of the saying, however. The other piece questions whether the impact, power, and functionality of a tree are at all meaningful if those qualities have no audience. Do those qualities matter if they are not evident? This part of the adage is about visibility.

If you apply a leadership lens, the answer to whether the tree makes a sound is a definite and deafening—no. If no one hears, sees, or feels the value you add to the organization, the answer to whether your leadership *makes a sound* is also a definite no. Without visibility, your leadership isn't there. It makes no sound. There is no tree. The end.

Through the lenses of competency and visibility—the two masks that can keep your leadership capabilities hidden—let's look at the Nine again. "In Time Out," "Hamster Wheel," and "Fallen Star"—these are people who are struggling to *do* leadership; theirs is a deficiency of leadership competency. As yet, they don't know what the *theys* in their organization want to see to recognize them as leaders. Meanwhile, "Stuck on Assistant" and "Out of Sight," along with "Untitled," are people who may know how to lead, but due to their lack of visibility, their value is going unseen. That leaves "Overpass'd," "Battlefield Promotion," and "Golden Cage." When it comes to competency and visibility, these leaders could probably use a little bit of both.

Strategic Reflection No. 7

To make your leadership value evident, do you need more competency, more visibility, or both, and what are the signs?

_____

_____

_____

_____

_____

_____

_____

_____

_____

_____

_____

_____

_____

Getting Started

The most important thing to remember is that leadership causes an impact. People can see it and feel it. Leadership makes a sound. Invisible, silent, and meaningless leadership is no leadership at all. To be recognized as a leader in your organization, discover what competencies your organization values. Try them on. Walk them around. Break them in. Own them and make them yours.

In the simplest terms, the base elements of evident leadership are action and visibility. Choose or ask for stretch assignments, projects, and work-related extracurriculars (e.g., special teams, strategic work streams, boards, or committees) that afford you venues and opportunities to demonstrate competent action or action that yields a beneficial business result. But being busy isn't the same thing as being relevant. When possible, don't say yes to just anything. Say yes to activities that advance a clear strategic objective—and in a way that is visible or can be measured or observed. Just as making your leadership *relevant* relies on your impactful action, making leadership *evident* relies on visibility. The two constitute leadership in execution. The two constitute leadership *walking*.

PART II

YOUR LEADERSHIP UNLOCKED

"Leadership is action, not position."
—Donald McGannon,
broadcasting industry executive

Removing what masks your leadership qualities
is only half the battle. Now that you know your
leadership must be seen to be believed, give people
something to look at. And it has to be something they
will recognize as leadership by the way it moves.

Chapter 5

HOW LEADERSHIP DOES BUSINESS

What evident business value looks like

LEADERSHIP IS DISTINCTIVE. It walks a certain way; talks a certain way; thinks, relates, and engages in certain ways. There's something about leadership so viscerally clear that although it's resistant to a nice and tight definition, we would never confuse it with anything other than what it is. So when you look at yourself, and when the *theys* look at you, the question becomes, are you what leadership is? What we know for sure is that leadership ultimately results in visible, evident, and easily observable change and value. But what kind of *walk, talk, thinking, relating,* and *being* mark a leader, especially one who is well positioned for a next-level role at work?

First, A Look At The Total Package

Many organizations answer the question of *what leadership is* through their stated lists of desirable leadership competencies. But if your organization has articulated no such inventory, this chapter, as well as the two that follow, will provide the usual suspects: common leadership competencies, as well as the embedded behaviors, skills, and choices that are typically recognized and preferred by organizational decision makers. In most cases, organizations identify a mix of competencies that fall into three categories of value-added work:

1. **Leadership competencies that add business value**: behaviors that cumulatively cause positive business outcomes and results.

2. **Leadership competencies that add relationship value:** behaviors that cumulatively help build strategic partnerships and connections.

3. **Leadership competencies that add value through self-mastery:** behaviors that cumulatively optimize how you use yourself to advance organizational objectives.

Together, these competencies, in their respective categories, produce outcomes organizations highly value as contributing to their most fundamental motivators: surviving and thriving. The next section focuses on putting competencies that add business value into action; whereas in chapters 6 and 7, we'll see how leaders walk in the competencies that add relationship value and the value that rises from self-mastery. Look for the list of competencies that organizations want, the value the organization gets when you demonstrate them, and what you need to do to make these competencies evident and visible to the *theys* who are always watching.

Leadership Competencies That Add Business Value

Why does your organization exist? What does your organization do? Does it create something, sell something, fix something, or help someone? Whatever is at the core of what your organization does, your leadership must visibly add strategic value in ways that advance your business' fundamental reason for being.

Organizations want you to:

- Understand the industry or domain specifically and holistically.

- Create strategic plans and sound approaches that drive change.

- Ensure systems, processes, commitments, and products deliver as promised.

- Drive positive short- and long-term change and value.

Understanding the Industry or Domain Specifically and Holistically - How to Make it Visible:

- Maintain the required technical acumen and functional proficiencies.

- Apply a holistic grasp of the business to help engage the right processes and controls.

- Be watchful of market conditions that can create potential opportunities or risks.

- Study trends and the future business landscape, while interpreting the implications.

- See alignments and divergences between the organization's local and global business priorities.

- Help key stakeholders respond strategically to what you have observed or recommended.

The Value Organizations Get: The business acumen to solve problems, address challenges, and leverage opportunities.

Creating Strategic Plans and Sound Approaches That Drive Change - How to Make it Visible:

- Build a clear and realistic vision of the future state of the business.

- Create, differentiate, and balance applying strategic versus tactical approaches to meet goals.

- Apply sound and well-timed judgment to decision-making.

- Advocate, influence, or evangelize the vision to partners and key stakeholders to get their support.

- Set expectations around the timing of execution; apply urgency and patience when appropriate.

The Value Organizations Get: A vision and strategy to achieve business objectives.

Ensuring systems, processes, commitments, and products deliver as promised - How to Make it Visible:

- Look for flaws, threats, and inefficiencies; challenge ineffective systems and processes that don't work.

- Execute plans, emphasizing the activities that matter most.

- Use budget allocations, time, and other business resources wisely.

- Stimulate results by leveraging best and next practice, strategic tools, and technologies.

- Continuously drive for results.

- Create wins, advantages, or solutions for customers and other stakeholders.

The Value Organizations Get: Delivery of the promised value to customers and others with an interest in the organization's success.

Driving Positive Short- and Long-Term Change and Value - How to Make it Visible:

- Learn and course correct as new data emerges.

- Continuously seek and pursue creative ways to innovate.

- Help people transition to the new normal.

- Build processes to sustain the effectiveness of the change.

- Anticipate and prepare for future changes.

The Value Organizations Get: Focus on the right current and forward-looking business priorities.

An Insider Tip
Developing Subject-Matter Expertise

*Every industry and work domain is anchored by the-
ories, thinking, philosophies, central hypotheses,
and core models. Develop a library of the bodies
of knowledge that underpin your career industry.
Collecting traditionally printed or digital books is
fine because those theories tend to remain static.
What is dynamic is the application of those theories. Application, or how the hypotheses are put
to practical use, changes often and fast. You can
more likely find and keep up with changing application through industry periodicals, serious trade
bloggers, industry futurists, business conventions,
think tanks, LinkedIn groups, and professional as-
sociations. These sources can be more transient,
but again, the data they offer are always fluid.*

*Another good source of study is your
company's peer group of competitors. These
peer companies are organizations that are similar
to yours in size, customer demographics, and
offerings. They grapple with the same challenges,
are looking for the same kinds of clients, and want
to achieve the same success objectives. What will
differentiate your company, and the others, is
often the how. Everyone's a teacher; some teach
you what to do, whereas others teach you what
not to do. Look for patterns relative to how your*

organization's peer companies operate. Glean insight from your observations because they are running the same race your organization is.

As your acumen grows, the work will shift to you being able to communicate what you have learned. Be generous with your knowledge. Anywhere it is useful and relevant, give it away. But be mindful of the gap between the amount of need-to-know information your audience requires, and the amount of interesting-to-know information you have between your ears. Typically what your audience needs is far less than what you can offer.

Learn how to engineer the communication vehicles found in the average workplace: decks, executive summaries, one-sheets, whitepapers, case studies, and proposals. You can find templates for these things online. However, tweak the template according to your organization's preferred style nuances.

Every one of the strategic behaviors discussed in this chapter can be supersized or reduced to fit the scope of your role. Remember our case studies subjects?

Case Study: Petra, Trey, Jacob, and Kat

Petra, a market development director, caused change by recognizing the opportunity to perform strategic outreach to an untapped market in the community. Trey, a senior project manager in IT, caused change by challenging the status quo of a deeply embedded but flawed system within the organization. Jacob, a senior client specialist in customer service, caused change by helping his customer adjust to the new normal. Kat, an analyst in finance, caused change by course correcting her own communication style to reduce its negative impact on the flow of work.

No matter the size and reach of the positive change you cause, it must add evident value to how your organization does business.

Strategic Reflection No. 8

Which competency behaviors do you recognize as helping you create business value? List three to five specific behaviors from this chapter that would help you further upgrade how you manifest those competencies in your role at work.

_____

_____

_____

Chapter 6

HOW LEADERSHIP RELATES

What evident relationship value looks like

Think of all the ways you can add business value as noted in the previous chapter. You can add value by understanding your business, creating a vision, taking good care of your clients, and advancing your business toward an aspired vision and beyond. But for all the ways you can bring positive change to your organization, not one is achievable entirely on your own. Each one requires the knowledge, time, talent, effort, acceptance, assistance, audience, or buy-in of others. Yes, leaders cause change, but only as a result of influencing the people around them. Your effectiveness as a leader echoes through and with those around you. The response you get from others is a direct reflection of your leadership's walk and talk. Without others, there's no leadership; you're just a metaphorical tree in a hypothetical forest, making no sound, causing no impact—and that equates to no leadership.

For the subjects of our case studies, let's look at how their leadership emerges from their influence and leveraged relationships.

Case Study:
Petra, Director of Market Development

To cause a change that added value, Petra first had to influence others. She engaged her team in building a sound and convincing business case, which she presented to the executive decision makers.

Initially, not many in the organization thought that building sites in an underserved part of town was a wise investment. But Petra had gone there with her team, built vital relationships, and got people talking so that she could learn about their needs, as well as the market potential, firsthand. The interviews she and her team conducted paid off and broke open one of the best-kept secrets in the city. This was a viable community and a potentially vibrant market; it was merely untapped.

Building offices in this community would be a win-win for the organization and the neighborhood. Now that Petra's proposal had won approval, she and the team needed to evangelize the same business case around the organization. They had to change everyone's impression of this market and help ready the enterprise for the new community of customers.

Case Study:
Trey, Senior Project Manager and Subject-Matter Expert, Information Technology

To cause a change that added value, Trey first had to influence others. He invited a cross-functional team of subject-matter experts from partner divisions to contribute to his work stream.

Although the success of the project was ultimately Trey's responsibility, the system operated using an intricate web of components, platforms, clouds, hardware, and software managed by other people, so there was no way he could go it alone. Not only were there a lot of moving parts, but the legacy system was also something of a sacred cow—a leftover from the legacy company consumed in a previous subsidiary merger. There was nothing magic about it; employees just didn't know anything else, so not only would he need technicians but also communicators to socialize the new system around the organization.

It was Trey's job, through this team, to build and transition everyone to something new and better. That was the long-term problem. The short-term challenge was that all the people Trey had recruited for this team had day jobs; they worked in several other areas of the organization. In addition to the expertise the team members would lend to this project, they each had a full plate of their usual assignments waiting at their desks. Having no formal authority over them, Trey would need to perform a balancing act: hold these committee members accountable while also keeping them, as volunteers, engaged in what for many would seem like a second job.

Case Study:
Jacob, Senior Client Specialist,
Customer Service

To cause a change that added value, Jacob first needed to influence others. He braced himself to hear out the customer on the phone, who was hostile and set on delivering a long-winded tirade.

She must have gone on and on for ten minutes, irately explaining that she had been a decades-long customer and preferred the company the way it used to be, along with the fact that she knew this executive partner and that market president. Left and right, she dropped the names of high-powered people in the company. The tactic was annoying, but it was nothing new: using the names of people with internal star power to scare the person on the line into compliance.

Although her freak-out was tedious, as Jacob listened, he found she had a point. The company had dramatically changed the look of the statements, without much notice to the customers or support for the employees to field these calls from people who had been taken by surprise. The new statements were difficult to read, Jacob empathized, especially if one were a senior who was used to her account statements looking a certain way for the past twenty years. He felt for her. So in response to her threatening to take her business to a competitor, Jacob asked her, although he personally had done nothing wrong, if he could have the opportunity to make it right.

Case Study:
Kat, Finance Analyst

To cause a change that added value, Kat would first need to influence others. Although her instincts were to defend herself, Kat listened beyond the sting of her manager's feedback, through which she learned that her communication style was landing the wrong way with her peers and partners. Although she was tactically strong—the strongest, in fact—others found her snarky, sarcastic, and offensive. More than an interpersonal issue, the resentment resulting from

Kat's manner was making others resistant to working with her, which was a direct threat to a group whose effectiveness relied on its ability to work smoothly as a team.

Kat had to change, and for her, it was more than a matter of bending to her boss' will or saving face. In truth, Kat loved the idea of being seen as the strongest contributor on the team, especially because she was among the most senior. Her long tenure gave her unique knowledge and a unique opportunity to be the go-to person. Secretly, that was precisely what she wanted. As informal as it may have been, it could give her a role of importance, one she would lose if she proved to be the bottleneck through which the work couldn't pass. Her wish would never materialize if no one trusted her. Kat knew things couldn't remain as they were. Although the cost might be her pride, she had to work to rebuild the interpersonal bridges between herself and the team.

Leadership Competencies That Add Relationship Value

As the cliché says, no one is an island. Whether your organization is a mega-enterprise, a midsize company, or a small start-up, it runs on the cooperation between people. Critical to being seen as a leader is your ability to visibly add value through building, maintaining, and leveraging strategic relationships.

Organizations want you to:

- Work actively to create diversity, inclusion, and belonging.

- Prioritize understanding and being understood by others.

- Connect with others in ways that optimize engagement and performance.

Working Actively to Create Diversity, Inclusion, and Belonging - How to Make it Visible:

- Challenge limiting beliefs about different people and their divergent perspectives.

- Be intentional about inviting a variety of viewpoints to inform and influence the work.

- Leverage diversity when making critical decisions, problem solving, and innovating.

- Facilitate an environment in which everyone has a valued and meaningful role in the work.

The Value Organizations Get: Access to diverse and engaged talent and stakeholders to build and advance the best business results.

Prioritizing Understanding and Being Understood by Others - How to Make it Visible:

- Practice emotional intelligence to foster productive work relationships.

- Recognize and respect the readiness of others to be influenced by a different line of thought.

- Create a compelling case that inspires partnership, alignment, cooperation, action, and followership.

- Support dialogue that facilitates mutual understanding.

- Listen actively, listen to understand, and communicate with purpose and clarity.

- Remain engaged and fully present when interacting with other people.

The Value Organizations Get: Effective communication that positively engages others as partners in the work.

Connecting with Others in Ways That Optimize Engagement and Performance - How to Make it Visible:

- Cooperate toward outcomes that offer mutual benefit.

- Develop others toward growth and achievement.

- Provide recognition and give credit where it's due.

- Navigate political realities with ethics.

- Negotiate and leverage conflict constructively and as a way to create the best results.

The Value Organizations Get: Engaged and highly skilled teams of people who get things done.

Strategic Reflection No. 9

Think about your last big win at work. In what ways did you need the cooperation of others? Which of the behaviors mentioned in this chapter did you practice? Has there ever been a time when you were able to deliver a great result completely in isolation and on your own?

_____

_____

_____

_____

_____

_____

Networking And Nails

Despite having human interactions all day and every day, for many people, formal networking is not as easy as it sounds. We all understand the virtues of it. A key ingredient of your workplace success story is your ability to form and leverage strategic relationships up, down, and sideways to ultimately cause change and value. Nothing—but nothing gets done in isolation. The *why* is the easy part.

It's the *how* that's problematic. Some people are introverted or their nerves get in the way. A sea of strange folks milling around a big room can be overwhelming, overstimulating, and can make some people feel as if they are in way over their heads. Others are put off by the misconception that you have to *work the room* in that tacky, "salesy" sort-of way. Who wants to be that opportunistic person who talks too much, too loud, with an overused line? And some of us just keep forgetting our business cards.

Personally, I hated networking—at least the way I used to define it. It was always the same painful ritual… I walk into the venue. It's alive with activity. There's cheap wine and crudité, and a line at the bar. Piped-in music is relaxing the after-work crowd. Several clusters of people are gathered buzzing with conversation. They are standing in a warm and friendly circle of familiarity. They are actively engaged in what looks like an interesting and enjoyable conversation. I start thinking about a not-so awkward way of awkwardly wedging myself in among them. I'd rather walk on a bed of nails than to insert myself, but I settle for walking to my car and going home, in truth, relieved—and a little defeated. It's a typical scene and a seemingly insurmountable obstacle to a social mechanism that most of us know is important to any business success. But what am I, and other nail walkers supposed to do? #networkingproblems. #thestruggleisreal.

Luckily with experience comes—well, new experiences, and the life lesson that there is always more than one way to sheer a sheep, peel an orange, cook an egg, or tackle the challenge of getting and keeping a healthy flow of new business connections in your life.

An Insider Tip
Are You a Hunter, Farmer, or Performer?

A common approach to networking is hunting. Whether the bounty is a new set of contacts, leads, or business cards, the hunter's modus operandi is to acquire business relationships by gathering. This is the kind of networking that occurs at mixers, conventions, large or all-hands meetings, or dedicated networking events. And that's why traditional networking events work well for hunters—there is an open field of prospects. The hunter needs merely to go bag 'em. However, if you prefer to grow your relationships more deliberately, instead of hunting, farm.

Farming is a mutualistic approach where you, the farmer, acquire relationships by individual cultivation, over a common area of interest and over time. Here, driving your networking effort is the desire to be of service, to learn, or to co-create an opportunity that serves you both. Farming can occur anywhere and with nearly anyone. Over the office bagels or via a friend of a friend, you meet someone who's engaged in something interesting. Or maybe you are only loosely connected. I once came across a local businesswoman on Facebook and began following her. Though we had different specialties, I liked the way she used social media to advance her brand. One day, I decided to direct-message her. I introduced myself, lauded her business approach, and invited her to coffee. We met and had a great conversation. I was happy to give her some new ideas, and I certainly learned some. Maybe you want to hear their story, or perhaps, you want to explore if there are any alignments in your respective work. Maybe there is a resource you can offer to help their efforts. A simple, "Your project sounds super interesting; may I buy you a coffee to learn how I can help?" can open up amazing opportunities you would only have access to through other people.

Performing is yet another way to draw people into your network. The performer attracts business relationships via demonstration and social proof. Based on the premise that the proof is in the pudding, this method of networking occurs when you look for (or create) venues to demonstrate what you can do in front of a selected audience who may require it at some point in the future. You, as the performer, are willing to offer some value upfront, via your performance, when you are confident it will spark a deep and enduring interest in the onlookers, who, in turn, may seek the offer later or refer you to others who will. Performers rely on social proof as the magnet that draws opportunity. The thinking is: If they see what I can do (or hear from *others who have), they will come; hence, speakers and facilitators commonly use this method. They show their value at meetings, seminars, keynotes, or on expert panels. Burgeoning organizational thought leaders and internal consultants also use this method. They demonstrate the usefulness of their acumen in front of an audience to build a reputation that can be leveraged into an opportunity later on. Crucial to this method of networking is an impactful performance that will endure over time, a way to keep your name and face in front of this audience beyond the particular performance, as well as a reliable and consistent method for your prospects to contact you when your offer is needed.*

Hunting is a legitimate approach to networking. However, equally viable are farming and performing—where you can convert a cultivated relationship, or your demonstrated ability to deliver, into something mutually beneficial for you and your new networked connections.

I haven't been in a big room full of strangers with no business cards in years. But, I love coffee, and have met many interesting people who would become good friends, colleagues, and business partners. Anymore, I pass on the cheap wine and piped-in music and perform now—so I can leverage those relationships later. And the mingling afterward? It's not so bad. I found a way of networking that is compatible with my style. The point is to build business relationships, from which you can take and give. Once you wrap your head around the *what*, and your style of making a connection, you can stress less about the *how*.

Leadership is about creating positive change, and that is only possible through connection with others. To cause evident value, the *theys* must see you cultivate relationships that mutually serve your needs and the needs of others. They must see you working to understand and be understood. And they must see you convert all that into the successful execution of the organization's priorities. However, you can't lead with and through others if you haven't mastered the most powerful leadership element of them all. Without it, everything you have read is moot, and all you have yet to read is an impossibility. Want a hint? Look in the mirror.

Chapter 7

HOW LEADERSHIP MANAGES WHAT MATTERS MOST

What the value of evident self-mastery looks like

RELATIONSHIP COMPETENCIES ARE critical to your success as a leader. In your organization, the ultimate outcome of a leader is to cause change that adds value. You know that to do this, you must engage others. And to engage others, you must master the most potent and vital leadership instrument of all: you. When it comes to making change and value happen, your presence is the most powerful leadership catalyst there is.

Molecules and Mack Trucks

Wielding the potency of your presence doesn't require much effort at all. You walk into the room, and the molecules start moving around. Just by showing up, you change the environment, the molecules, and much more. You've likely seen this power before as it plays out every day in offices everywhere. A certain someone arrives in the office, and the whole mood changes. The atmosphere is lighter and pleasant. Sunshine, daisies, and bluebirds appear. And then a certain someone else walks in, and suddenly it's thunderstorms, hail, and hellfire from the sky. Sun or storm, presence is powerful.

It likely all happens accidentally. That certain someone and that certain someone else are probably causing these seismic shifts in the room without their even meaning to. It is likely all happening outside their awareness and without intention. They aren't trying to affect the room; they're just showing up. Consider how much power that is, the ability to change the emotional temperature and disposition of separate and fully formed human beings without touching them or saying a word. Just. By. Showing. Up. That certain someone and that certain someone else are just doing what each one does, bringing heaven and bringing hell, all without strategic planning or forethought. Both are impacting the environment just by stepping into it.

Imagine if these two did what they are capable of doing on purpose. Imagine the force of intention entering with each one. Imagine the beauty. Imagine the pain. Imagine, if each one was armed with awareness and purpose, what dreams and nightmares may come. That's how powerful *your* presence is. It doesn't even require your awareness to do what it does. However, though powerful, it's not leadership. Powerful presence alone is not leadership. For your presence to translate as your evident capacity to lead, it must be tempered by your self-mastery.

Self-mastery is made up of three parts: self-awareness, self-management, and versatility, or the ability and willingness to adapt. Of these, the most essential is self-awareness. Self-awareness, or simply you understanding you, is the first and most crucial building block of leadership. Of all the complex operations a leader might manage, why is something as simple as understanding oneself so critical? The fact is, you are as impactful, powerful, potent, intricate, and complex as a massive and muscular Mack truck. That's right; when it comes to you being able to affect change in your environment, you are a forty-ton eighteen-wheeler. But imagine driving that much machine with little or no understanding of how it works. Imagine barreling down the highway, powered by the speed and strength of that monster truck, and you with no license to drive. Imagine trying to maneuver the velocity and enormity of it around twists and turns and change, clueless about the controls. The result is easy to predict: a great big sloppy mess of steel, blood, and guts.

Self-awareness is your license to drive and operate all the power inherent in you. Understanding and mastering the powerful and sophisticated machinery that you are is directly reflected in your ability to influence other people and the direction of circumstances, and through these, cause positive change at work. To be seen as a leader in your organization, you must use yourself well. You must use yourself well to drive the business from here to there. You must use yourself well to build relationships and, through them, get things done. But how do you put to good use a force you scarcely understand?

This or That?

Like all things, human beings are full of polarity: yin and yang, flaws and virtues, potentials and limitations, the good and the bad, the beautiful and the ugly. Once you understand your full inventory of characteristics, you can have something that is arguably unique to us as a species: strategic choice versus enslavement to compulsions, instincts, and habits. When you understand the full range of what you are capable of, you can choose. When confronted by a distressful situation at work, you can choose to activate this characteristic or that one, that strength or this one. Without awareness, however, there is no choice, only your knee-jerk reactions, only your feral instincts.

When you consider all the stressful potentialities that can happen during the average day in the life of a leader, it isn't difficult to understand why you can't be asleep at the wheel. A person who operates outside of self-awareness is one who is, in fact, asleep in that he or she is leading by subconsciously triggered habits and thoughtless impulses. They say, as long as you have choices, you're a wealthy person. But relative to your ability to solve problems as a leader, your sleep state reduces your choices to the "four basic defense structures," or the Four Fs, as described by psychotherapist and trauma-typology expert Peter Walker.

Left to our own instincts, the amygdala, one of the oldest and most unevolved parts of the human brain, serves as one of the body's emergency alert systems, putting four options on our menu in response to stress and duress: fight, flight, freeze, and appease.[18] Doing battle at work, or *fighting*, may look like getting defensive when you have just been given critical performance feedback you didn't want to hear. Running away at work, or *fleeing*, could mean saying no to a stretch assignment meant to grow your ability just because it dauntingly sits outside your comfort zone. Standing still at work, or *freezing*, might look like you opting for silence versus offering up a unique idea for fear of looking silly in a team meeting. Kissing up at work, or *fawning*, might include choosing to flower up feedback when your employee needs to know the truth about his or her disappointing production numbers.

Self-awareness, then, is recognizing the truth about ourselves, no matter how cringe-worthy or unappealing it may be. It's recognizing that you are about to protect your bruised ego by putting up an argumentative smoke screen rather than admitting your performance is lacking. It's acknowledging that you're about to choose the status quo because you're afraid of the first awkward and scary steps toward something new. It's knowing you are choosing to silence a sound business idea to save face in front of your boss and peers. And it's seeing the fact that you are about to choose being liked over being a good coach to an employee who needs the truth about his or her performance. Self-awareness is you telling yourself the truth even when it's not pretty. So why do it? The truth will set you free. The truth of self-awareness will set the leader you really are free. Yes, the truth costs. It costs pain and discomfort. However, it also buys something: choice and the power to self-manage.

Without self-awareness, we are more likely to make choices reliant on our habits, reflexes, imagined fears, shame, and animal instincts. With self-awareness, we can "human-up" and choose. You can choose to protect your ego and dispute the feedback, or you can listen and potentially learn. You can choose the safe and same ol' assignments, or you can discover what's possible by challenging your abilities. You can choose to be a silent spectator, or you can offer a new, well-considered, and well-timed idea. You can choose to wear a smiling face and sidestep a difficult conversation, or you can tell the difficult truth while there's still time to help an employee course correct.

With the truth in play, now you can make a strategic choice. That is how self-awareness evolves into self-management. Recognizing the truth about yourself, along with making a conscious and strategic decision that is informed by wanting to demonstrate evident leadership, is where self-awareness becomes self-management. From here, self-mastery is only a few steps away.

Gaps and Gripes

To accelerate a leader's self-awareness and, with it, the leader's self-management, executive coaches like me will often use a 360-degree assessment—a tool that helps the subject understand how his or her leadership characteristics are experienced and perceived, not only through the subject's own eyes but also through the eyes of others. Everyone gets a say because the tool draws self-reported data from the subject him- or herself, as well as data from the subject's manager above, employees below, and peers alongside—hence the name: 360-degree assessment. Any gaps between the subject's perception of his or her own leadership, and that of the other respondents, signifies leadership development gold. That's because gaps in perception are, in fact, gaps in the subject's self-awareness. It means that when it comes to whether the subject demonstrates a particular leadership competency, the subject and their respondents disagree—and there is usually a great deal to learn from that disagreement. Such 360-degree assessments, accompanied by coaching, serve the goal of raising a leader's awareness of how others experience his or her leadership characteristics, while also helping the coach apply growth strategies where they will do the most good. Why build all leadership muscles when the assessment results can point to and prioritize the most critical on which to focus a development strategy?

Although I regularly use feedback instruments like these in my practice, I do have my pet peeves. In assessment work, *weaknesses* is the term usually given to characteristics that are at the center of a gap occurring between the subject's and the other respondents' perceptions. Weaknesses are, of course, undesirable, and a great deal of energy goes toward reducing or eliminating them through the development process, as if they were big, ugly warts that require surgical removal. This binary lens of strengths/weaknesses frustrates me; it is a limiting way to see one's complexity, warts and all. Polarity notwithstanding, the word *weaknesses* is, in my opinion, a deceptively simple, black-and-white kind of term, especially for those wanting to lead effectively in a world with innumerable shades of gray.

Let's say I am left-handed. Because I use my left hand for most operations, it's naturally stronger than my right. On the basis that weaknesses should be reduced or eliminated, does that mean I should work to reduce or eliminate my right hand? *I don't think so—not with this manicure!* Although my right hand is weaker along the metric of tactile strength, there are still tasks that are perfectly served or assisted by its presence. So in truth, part of what makes my right hand weak is not so much its physical condition as compared to my left, but the situations in which I'm trying to use it. There are some circumstances in which my right hand is flawlessly suited for the task.

There are other cases, however, where my right hand indeed requires the help of its stronger twin, my left—but not always. A weakness in one instance isn't necessarily a weakness in all instances. So should one eliminate a characteristic deemed as a weakness? Or should one be more conscientious about the situations in which a characteristic is applied? Are characteristics deemed strengths truly and always *all that and a bag of chips?* No. Strengths, too, can be weaknesses when they are overplayed, underplayed, or played at the wrong time. All this is moot, however, if you don't know what you're working with. So one gift of self-awareness is its allowance for you to be your *whole self*—with the understanding that your assortment of attributes may serve you differently, for better or for worse, from situation to situation.

Hang on—because self-awareness isn't finished giving its gifts—not by a long shot. Imagine that the strength in my left hand was entirely out of my awareness. I have a strong and capable left hand, but by some amnesia, I don't know anything about it. What if this strong left hand was entirely in my blind spot? Without the awareness of this particular strength, I am forced to use my weaker right hand. Without the awareness of my strong lefty, I am forced to awkwardly negotiate this task and that task with my weaker right. Imagine the burden. Although my right hand may ultimately improve and rise to the occasion, with how many basic operations must I struggle, not for lack of the strength—because I possess it in my left hand—but for lack of knowledge of it? How much time and effort will be wasted grabbling with my weaker self when my strength is right there, waiting just outside my awareness? What could I accomplish if I knew my strength and relief were merely an appendage away?

So you see, it is not the weakness itself that is the weakness; the weakness is that my strengths are buried deep in my potential. This hidden potential, in which my strength is unknown, is the weakness. A strength you don't know you possess is as good as not having that strength at all. If you don't know about it, you can't activate it when you need to. Self-awareness generously gives you choices, options, strengths, and resources. It pulls these things into your line of sight, where you can manage them as you need to. Without self-awareness, a treasure chest of potential strengths sits waiting to be discovered and put to good use.

Versatility

With self-awareness, leaders have more options when it comes to operating in the world. These leaders are more versatile. Versatility, the ability to adapt skills and approaches to fit different contexts... the ability to have more than one way of getting things done, is the ultimate gift of self-awareness and self-management. With fuller self-awareness, you are not bound to your defense mechanisms, animal instincts, impulses, and habits. You don't have to do something just because that's what you do or have always done. With self-awareness, you can make a different choice.

You know that you cannot maximize what you, as a leader, are capable of without moving the will of people and the direction of circumstances. Versatility is the key to influencing a broad and diverse group of people and situations. Through versatility, you can choose the most effective way of reaching the people who will help you cause change and add value. What will influence one person won't necessarily influence another. You need an assortment of characteristics from your inventory to have a broad range of influence. When self-awareness, self-management, and versatility, or the willingness and ability to adapt, come together, the result is self-mastered leaders who can be themselves *on purpose* and *with purpose*, across a variety of circumstances, allowing those leaders to influence a broad spectrum of people. How did the subjects of our case studies demonstrate self-mastery? How did it help them influence the people around them, with and through whom they ultimately produced positive change?

Case Study:
Petra, Director of Market Development

That Petra's employees would follow her any-where was no surprise as most everyone who met her was energized by her passionate and big-picture thinking. Her team's deep engagement and commitment to her was a natural result of Petra's ability to make the vision seem so exciting, so real, and so achievable. Petra knew selling big ideas was her sweet spot, but she also understood that she, with her personality on full throttle, wasn't everybody's cup of tea. To some, her style could seem grandiose, dynamic, and not bound by the laws of gravity and the real world. Although in her gut and heart she excitedly knew her idea of building a presence in an underserved part of town was the right thing for the community and the business, she decided to remain staid, fact based, serious, and strategic in how she pitched her business case to a typically conservative and risk-averse group of executives.

Case Study:
Trey, Senior Project Manager, Information Technology

What Trey, a seasoned "tech geek," loved most about his job was his autonomy and independence. He was perfectly content working on his algorithms and systems and only interacting with others through the buffer of technology and only when necessary. So when it was necessary, people found him to be serious, stoic, and a give-it-to-them-straight kind of guy. That, along with his analytical manner, was part of what made him effective and credible in his IT position.

However, in this new situation, where he would be leading a significant work stream that engaged many subject-matter experts from other parts of the organization, Trey had to remember that the people working with him were not his to boss around. These were his peers. They were all still responsible for doing their day jobs; and Trey didn't have the "teeth" some managers use to get compliance. Maybe he didn't need that strategy, he considered. Maybe if he treated them like collaborators, thought leaders, and equal partners in birthing his idea, he could get something out of them that was way more valuable: their commitment.

Case Study: Jacob, Senior Client Specialist, Customer Service

Although Jacob was slow to anger, he knew that if pushed, he could give as good as he got. And boy, was this customer pushing! Although parts of him wanted to unleash his frustration at the angry customer on the line, Jacob remained still, choosing instead to focus on the fact that she was upset at the process and not with him. When he listened beyond her ranting, he could hear a person who was simply frustrated because the changes to the statement had come with no warning and no support.

But he heard something else too: worry and fear. To this longtime customer, an elderly but highly independent widow, the changes had been jarring. He could understand why, especially given his impression of her as someone who prized her ability to still manage her own business affairs. He imagined that her inability to make sense of the form might have shaken that confidence. Jacob knew he had the option of saying, "Good luck with this... hope you work that whole crazy-looking statement thing out!" And at various times during the difficult conversation, that's precisely what he wanted to do. But that wouldn't calm her or convince her to keep her business with the company, which he also wanted. Only restoring the customer's confidence and comfort level would do that.

Case Study: Kat, Finance Analyst

One of the development methods Kat's manager had suggested was getting 360-degree feedback so that she could clearly understand what behaviors, from the perspective of her coworkers, were killing her effectiveness on the team. However, that was easier said than done. Kat's interpersonal style had hurt her relationships with her coworkers so much that they were initially afraid to tell her anything. That in itself was feedback. The fact that her coworkers refused to communicate with her, even anonymously through an instrument, was data. Even though each person's responses would be scrubbed and combined with the responses of others, their insistent silence spoke volumes.

Although it took repeated reassurances from her manager, Kat's peers finally eked out just enough feedback in the report to confirm what the manager had already told her: Kat's snark and sarcasm had damaged her peer relationships. As Kat continued to read the report's narrative, a clear message emerged. Even though her respondents fully recognized the benefits of Kat's long tenure, experience, and knowledge, it was moot because they simply didn't want to ask her for help. The bad attitude that generally came with her assistance was too high a price to pay— even for a right answer.

How was Kat supposed to climb to the status of SME or go-to person if her team members couldn't talk to her? The answer was, she wouldn't. The truth was plain and looking her right in the face. As Kat stood to leave the meeting with the weight of the assessment results still hanging in the air, her manager gave her a warning: "I need you to watch it," he began, "now more than ever. We invited everyone to give you honest feedback on this assessment; don't, through your attitude, punish them for doing what we asked them to do." Although her manager's words stung, Kat knew the warning was a wise one and, based on her past behavior, deserved. What Kat did next, however, came as a big surprise to everyone—even, in a way, to Kat, herself. The email she sent to the whole team read as follows: Hey everyone.... just a note to thank you for doing the assessment. I know I haven't made it easy to communicate with me. All of this is part of a plan I'm working on to change that. You know me. Ordinarily I would just walk up and say what was on my mind, but considering some of the mistakes I've made, I thought a note wouldn't be as pushy .... see, I'm learning already.

I won't lie: reading the report wasn't easy. But I did read it, and it's sinking in. I didn't know the effect I was having on many of you. I had no idea. I thought I was being funny... but in reality, I've learned, I was being hurtful.

I wanted to tell you that I'm serious about making some changes. I might even come to a few of you for help on a couple of specifics. It's not to corner you or anything. I just might need some more details. I'm a thousand percent sure I'm gonna to make some mistakes. So please be patient as I work on being a better teammate. It's something I really want to do. And can do—with your help. Thanks again, Kat.

Leadership Competencies That Add Value through Self-Mastery

These are the most fundamental to your leadership success: the behaviors that activate your best self as dictated by the situation at hand. Yours is a vast inventory of characteristics that can create countless outcomes, or no outcome at all, especially if you cannot harness all that you are. To add visible leadership value with and through others at work, you must use yourself well.

Organizations want you to:

- Increase self-awareness continuously.

- Maintain self-control in a variety of situations.

- Adapt and adjust situationally while remaining effective.

Increasing Self-Awareness Continuously - How to Make it Visible:

- Regularly engage in activities that provide insights and feedback to broaden self-knowledge.

- Acknowledge strengths and areas for improvement.

- Embrace development opportunities and experiences that encourage learning and skill growth.

- Monitor impact and calibrate as you change and grow long-term.

- Build your expertise and brand as a reliable partner, credible manager, or trusted advisor.

The Value Organizations Get: Leadership talent that can learn and positively evolve.

Maintaining Self-Control in a Variety of Situations - How to Make it Visible:

- Be appropriately transparent with your thoughts, feelings, and motivations.
- Behave in ways that align with your stated beliefs and convictions.
- Model your company's values in your ethics, behaviors, choices, and decision-making.
- Be accountable for the results that arise from your areas of responsibility.
- Project poise, credibility, courage, and confidence in dynamic circumstances.
- Express passion, enthusiasm, and energy appropriate to the circumstance.
- Demonstrate command to gain the confidence and followership of others.
- Show respect to build trust.

The Value Organizations Get: Leadership talent that can self-regulate.

Adapting and Adjusting Situationally while Remaining Effective - How to Make it Visible:

- Be intentional and operate with purpose.

- Adjust your communication and behavioral style to best influence and connect with the current audience.

- Read the situation to inform the appropriateness of what to do or say next.

- Be flexible to the needs of others while remaining authentic.

- Maintain focus, endurance, resilience, and sound judgment during delay, change, ambiguity, stress, or crisis.

The Value Organizations Get: Leadership talent that is effective in dynamic business situations.

Strategic Reflection No. 10

Think about a time when you had to exhibit self-mastery to cause the desired impact. How did self-managing help you influence others or the situation? What would have been the consequences had you chosen not to self-manage?

_____

_____

_____

_____

_____

_____

Do You

Everyone is just like you. Some are just like you. No one is just like you. In graduate school, I first encountered this string of seemingly contradictory lines that demonstrate the paradoxical and coexisting realities of diversity. You are a human being and, in that way, like everyone else. You have a community, a workplace, a department, and a role, all of which make you like some but unlike others. Finally, when your race, gender, region, education, sexuality, talents, and an infinite list of other herbs and spices come together to compose your distinctive recipe, you will find that you are unique in all the world.

Although more than fifty competency behaviors are listed in the preceding pages, each one is hollow. They are generic, unbranded, and only vaguely resemble how they will play out in real life. When practically applied, every straightforward behavior noted in these pages is nuanced according to you, the unique leader, who is like everyone else, only like some, and simultaneously like no one else in the world. Do not mistake these competency behaviors as advocacy for cookie-cutter leadership. As a unique human being, you will manifest your version of each of them. No two leaders will do any competency identically—and from an organizational effectiveness standpoint, thank heaven!

Imagine a department of people who were all the same, a work group full of clones. They are all competent, but faceless, colorless, and *uniquenessless*. In some ways, these clones are on easy street; after all, they would all share the same understanding, knowledge, memories, perspectives, and strengths. There's no conflict because our clones all share the same lens through which they see and experience the world. As our clones merrily go off to work, they can look forward to nothing but smooth sailing, right? Wrong! Although a homogeneous group shares the same strengths, these individuals also share similar frailties and limitations. They are all susceptible to the same threats. Because they all know nothing but the same thing, their shared understanding becomes their ceiling. Their similarity is the imprisoning limit of what they collectively know.

In diversity, where a variety of leaders contribute an assortment of strengths, a given organization acquires a full, well-rounded, and well-stocked arsenal with which to do battle in a dynamic marketplace with plenty of tricks up its sleeve. Although the competencies indexed in this book give you a general and generic catalog of the behaviors organizations want to see in their leaders, informing your walk and talk of these anemic items should be your unique experience, perspective, and personhood. Many organizations value a standard slate of competencies by which to identify and promote their leaders. However, the most successful organizations hope that their most valued competencies are made manifest by diverse people, through whom the organization can negotiate an array of clients, threats, challenges, and opportunities in the marketplace. Leadership is something you have to do; it's an act. It's a choice. You have to *do* leadership; be sure to do it *your* way.

Bringing It All Together

In describing how a leader adds value, we have incidentally defined leadership as the following: a leader works toward self-mastery. Leaders understand themselves and can manage their attributes, knowing any of them can be a strength or a weakness given the circumstances. Leaders are versatile, knowing that they, themselves, are the most potent and vital instrument they have to influence others. Leaders engage and influence. Their self-awareness and self-management allow them to calibrate to and influence various circumstances and the diverse people therein, with and through whom they can actualize value the organization can see and feel. Leaders cause change and add value. Leaders know it is only through others that they can achieve an organizational change that creates a business advantage.

> **Leaders self-master, which allows them to effectively engage and influence others, with and through whom they can cause change that adds value.**

Notice this sequence of three key segments: self-mastery, engagement and influence, and causing change and value (see figure 1). That leadership is ordered in this way is no coincidence. Try googling "leadership." At the time I wrote this book, there were about 1.7 billion results on the subject. Nearly all of them will discuss influencing. In our socially networked world, nothing gets done without relationships. As a leader, despite your big brain and unique strengths, you will never be as smart or as strong as a team of people with equally big brains and diverse strengths working with you, beside you, or on your behalf toward a common goal. Harnessing that collective strength is the result of influence— your ability to inspire followership, your ability to move the will of others to give you the benefit of their time, talent, and energy. Influence is leadership's anchor, for good reason. It's a bridge. Without it, self-mastery becomes unnecessary. Without it, positive change becomes impossible.

Fig. 1. The Leadership Sequence

Strategic Reflection No. 11

The elements of the sequence act as links in a chain that ultimately result in you causing change and value at work, the origins of which will always take you back to the basis of leadership: self-mastery. Still in doubt? Reverse engineer it. Think of a recent professional win. In what ways did you cause change that added value? To achieve your success, who did you engage and influence? To gain the followership of those people, in what ways did you have to be self-mastered (adaptable, self-managing, and self-aware)?

_____

_____

_____

_____

_____

Although influence is the foundation of leadership, it is still reliant on what comes before and after it in the sequence. Keep influence at the center, but take away self-mastery. In other words, you rush into circumstance. You're raw, feral and uncalibrated, but you still manage to cause change and value. While success may come accidentally, it won't be sustainable. At best, it means you're an influential doer who has randomly tripped into success. Don't start celebrating; without self-awareness and self-management, you can't activate or replicate what worked on demand. That's not leadership, that's called luck.

This time, keep influence at the center but take away from the sequence causing change and value. You are self-aware, self-managing, and versatile. You can influence circumstance and people, but you yield no results. In this case, you might be a likable doer who cannot cause a relevant outcome. There's activity, but no change, nor value. Again, that's not leadership, that's called waste. There has been a lot of activity—with nothing to show for it. Leadership is the product of all three: self-mastery that enables the engagement and influence of others, with and through whom you cause change that adds value.

Important to note is the building of required visible competencies within the sequence (see figure 2). The lowest-order segment of the sequence, self-mastery, requires the lowest degree of visible competence. The segment of engaging and influencing others, however, takes more visible competence for it to begin resembling leadership. Causing change and value is the highest-order segment of the sequence because it requires the most visible competence. The increase of necessary competencies as you move through the sequence is nice and academic on paper, but how are these different stair steps experienced in real life? Ask Ethan, one of Trey's coworkers.

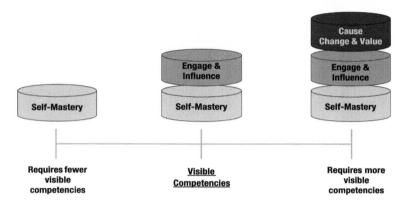

Fig. 2. Degree of Required Competence while Ascending the Leadership Sequence

Case Study:
Ethan, Senior Project Manager and SME, Information Technology

Like Trey, Ethan was in a position to parlay his skills into a next-level role in information technology (IT). Although you, Trey, and I know that any and all next-level positions require one to demonstrate leadership, apparently Ethan did not, or at least he didn't know enough. What he did know was IT. Ethan ate, drank, and breathed IT. He tracked the competitors and studied trends, as well as what was best and next in the industry. As soon as someone recognized all of his knowledge, Ethan surmised, it would be jet fuel for his career. In some respects, Ethan was demonstrating a higher-order behavior: building business acumen (from the leadership competencies that add business value). However, while Ethan was busy filling his brain, he was failing to do something else: open his mouth. Ethan never spoke up in meetings. He'd rather be silent than risk looking silly. He never used the acumen he was building; he didn't even share his insights with those who could have. Ethan's failure to self-master set up his inability to influence. These more basic building blocks of the sequence made his higher-order competence moot.

Then came an opportunity for Ethan to lead, when his work team was on the verge of making a serious error in strategic direction. If ever the team needed his business insights, it was then. Still, Ethan was silent, a prisoner of the slightest risk to his ego. He told himself it wasn't important anyhow; he was saving his business acumen for a real opportunity—like the kind that comes with a formal job interview. And Ethan was right. There wasn't a formal interview afoot with a panel of hiring managers looking on. But Ethan also was wrong. There was an interview of sorts—an informal *opportunity for Ethan to demonstrate evident leadership, and he let it slip through his fingers. How sad it was that even the higher-order business acumen was undermined by a failure of confidence, a lower-order element within the sequence. With these two parts of Ethan's sequence in conflict, even his highest-order competence didn't matter. He might as well not have had it at all.*

Experiment

In my coaching practice, I rarely send a client out committed to making a specific change. More often, I suggest experimenting. A course of action is an experiment when we are not sure what the outcome will be. When experimenting, we don't have to make a commitment. Experiments can be performed imperfectly, and adjustments can be made. If mistakes happen, we can just return to the table and try something else. In an experiment, we never fail; we only learn.

I also avoid sending my client out with a long laundry list of new behaviors to manage. I more often suggest that my client take one thing we've discussed and try it on just to see how it fits, just for a little while, and just to see what happens. I invite my client to pay attention to how he or she feels while experimenting with a new way of *doing* leadership. I invite him or her to evaluate what feels right and like it's *a keeper*, as well as what doesn't. What I don't do is allow my client to passively swallow ideas whole, blindly, and without consideration. Leaders don't do that; leaders think. Leaders choose.

An Insider Tip
Small Is Big; Slow Is Fast

This book is full of insights and strategies to help you demonstrate your ability as a competent and evident leader. But I should warn you. Trying all of these suggestions and strategies at once will cause failure—or at least exhaustion. This is chess, not checkers. The journey to being seen as a competent and evident leader is not a quick flight of fancy—it's a strategic journey. Start slow to go fast later. Small shifts can make a big impact.

1. *Choose one small shift at a time, only one, and not as a committed change but as an experiment.*

2. *Pay attention to how it feels as you test looking and thinking about the world through the lens of the reestablished, reimagined, or reinvented leader you are.*

3. *Specifically look at what happens or doesn't happen as a result of the single changed behavior. Was there an impact on your work, was there an effect on your relationships, or was the result seen and/or felt in you?*

The Chinese philosopher Lao Tzu wrote, "A journey of a thousand miles begins with one step." Which single step will be your first?

Getting Started

The Greek philosopher Socrates wrote, we should be as we wish to seem. What he meant was that we should walk, talk, and think like the leaders we wish to be. First, get clear on the fact that you are a leader. Leadership is not about title, rank, or pay scale. You will likely exhibit visible competencies and do leadership long before anyone formally calls you one. Before anyone else will see leadership ability in you, you must see it and be it—yourself. At the most fundamental level, leadership is being your best self so that you can engage and influence others, with and through whom you cause change that adds value in or for your organization. Every bit of that definition is within your control. The *theys* may decide who gets a formal promotion, but a promotion isn't required for you to be a leader. The *theys* may choose who receives an official title, but they cannot control the leader you see or are starting to see when you look in the mirror. The *theys* can't choose leadership for you; only you can do that.

Strategic Reflection No. 12

There's a proverb that says, "So a person thinks, so that person is." In the space provided, list five things you would do differently at work if you thought of yourself, regardless of your current job title, as a leader or a more senior-level leader. Then examine your list for those items that would be appropriate for your role and do not require formal authority or a promotion to execute. Those items are ways to demonstrate leadership, not by promotion or authority, but by your decision. Look at your list. In what ways is the decision the only thing stopping you from being the leader you really are?

1.

2.

3.

4.

5.

_____

_____

_____

_____

_____

Having examined the doing and the optics of evident leadership, you might ask, "Is that it? Is that all there is to leading?" In an academic sense, the answer is yes. In a pragmatic, real-world sense, will seeing yourself as one while walking and talking like one get you positively noticed as a leader at work? That's a yes too, or at least—a probably. But, will it, alone, take you to the end of the journey where you will more likely be seen and appreciated as the leader you really are? No. We have further to go, and be warned: the way isn't straight or simple. This leg of your leadership journey won't be as prescribed and formulaic as it has been so far. When it comes to leadership, sometimes you have to *feel* your way through. Leadership isn't just "science." In application, leadership is just as much "art."

PART III

YOUR LEADERSHIP UNLEASHED

"It is what you don't expect... that most needs looking for."

—Neal Stephenson, author of speculative fiction

You are walking steadily in the sequence. Now is the time for nuance, the not easily seen, and the almost indiscernible. Now that you have reinvented, the focus shifts to the faintest traces, to that which cannot be readily observed. Though small and subtle, they are the things that will set you apart and bring your leadership where it belongs—out into the light.

Chapter 8

LOCATION, LOCATION, LOCATION

Where leadership happens

FOR MANY PROFESSIONALS, finally understanding leadership is the find of their career: mastering self to engage and influence others, with and through whom you cause change that adds value. The equation of leadership is straightforward and easy to grasp. If only being lifted to the next level was that formulaic, but I'm afraid it's not. Some people are completely prepared to walk in the sequence. They are ready to step in each segment faithfully, and yet they will still fail. They will still struggle to bring their leadership capability out into the light, where it can be seen, appreciated, and rewarded. But why? Why, when it comes to the sequence, does one plus one plus one fail to equal the sum parts of evident leadership?

The Classics and Kitchen Knives

When I was a girl, my father, an English teacher and lover of the theater, would perform one-man shows in the kitchen. Using ordinary knives, plates, and colanders, my dad took me deep into the tales of *Oedipus Rex*, *Macbeth*, *Othello*, *Frankenstein*, and *Beowulf*, playing all the parts himself. It was hypnotic. *Hamlet* is still my favorite. It's got everything: ghosts, sex, murder, politics, romance, humor—everything. Even as I have evolved into the people-development business, *Hamlet* continues to prove instructive. There's one line I especially love. The depressed Danish prince is debating whether his homeland is like a confining prison. When others disagree, Hamlet says, "there is nothing either good or bad, but thinking makes it so."[19] Mr. Shakespeare, I don't mean to throw any shade, but when it comes to leadership, might I suggest one tiny edit? There is nothing either good or bad, but ~~thinking~~ *circumstance* makes it so.

Then there's my mom (*again*), who is famous for saying something along the same lines. It usually followed when I saw someone do something I found odd or inexplicable. Of course, I just *had* to comment because that's what the world needed—a piece of *my* mind. That's when I, a know-it-all and world-wise adolescent, declared with judgment and disgust, "I would never, ever do that... I would never—*in my entire life*—do that!" And my mother would look at me, in that way mothers do when they are about to skillfully demonstrate that you really don't know your butt from a hole in the ground! "Before it's all over," she'd say, smirking with wisdom and knowing, "I'll see you eat the leaves off the trees," meaning there was no telling what I might find right or necessary if the situation demanded it—so maybe I should keep my uninformed judgments to myself! And then came the parental lectures about being adaptable and versatile as one moves through life. Shakespeare's famous protagonist and my mom agree on the fact that rightness or appropriateness is relative and highly dependent on the situation in which you find yourself. Although I have yet to nosh on any leaves, thank heaven, I know this for sure: leadership and what's appropriate are matters of circumstance. *Dang!* She was right again.

This call for versatility doesn't mean you should be two-faced, false, or disingenuous. It's about being your best self in all situations, but because all situations vary, what is "best" will change. Your best self while springing to action to help a cherub-faced toddler out of the path of an oncoming Maserati would likely differ from your best self as you listen to a technical and sedate lecture on the life cycle of dung beetles. Whether it's moving at the speed of light or sitting staid and still, both courses of action, although vastly different, are appropriate responses relative to their circumstances. Situationally appropriate leadership is about calibration to the context at hand. It's about knowing what in you should be turned up, turned down, turned off, or all together *unplugged*.

Hi-Fi and H$_2$O

Leadership is fluid, situational, agile, and responsive to its context. Context is the stage on which leadership plays out. Context describes the dynamic conditions that form the setting in which leadership unfolds. Context informs how your leadership should show itself. That's simple enough, yes? It is, except that the contexts in which leadership happens are not created equally.

Although leadership still causes change and value, the contexts will dictate the exact degree of change, the variable definitions of value, and the innumerable and diverse people through which you must achieve both. The methods by which you cause that change will vary also. All contexts in which you demonstrate leadership will be unique in scope and expectation. Yet no matter the context, your leadership has to deliver.

Consider this famous quote by martial artist and actor Bruce Lee: "Empty your mind, be formless. Shapeless, like water. If you put water into a cup, it becomes the cup. You put water into a bottle and it becomes the bottle. You put it in a teapot it becomes the teapot. Now, water can flow or it can crash. Be water, my friend." The quote is pointing out that one must contract and expand relative to the situation. The water doesn't change; it only responds to the vessel in which it stands. Your leadership will not change either; it only responds to the situation in which you stand. Leadership doesn't have an on/off switch. Instead, think of the elements of your leadership as operating on dimmers so that each one can be tuned to the situation in play. You will still be expected to lead, just only in a way that is calibrated to the context at hand.

As a pimply-faced teenager of the 1980s, nothing was more cherished by me than my first stereo. It was the genesis of countless mixtapes—one for every preteen emotion and experience I had. A compact shelf unit, my beloved stereo had an equalizer plate with knobs controlling the treble, fade, and beatbox bass. Imagine that the behaviors making up your leadership competencies are the knobs on an equalizer deck. You can adjust your equalizer any way you wish, turning aspects of your leadership up or down.

Let's focus on one knob on your equalizer, "continuously seeking and pursuing creative ways to innovate," as an example. Always looking for ways to bring positive change is an attribute all good leaders have, so it should never be turned off. However, like all leadership qualities, it is subject to polarity. Even this competency behavior can, when taken alone and under the right conditions, have a strong and a frail side, have a light and a dark side, and be a virtue or a shadow. There are times when it can be overplayed, turned too far up, as in pursuing more change at the close of a complex initiative when people are fatigued and looking for stability. And it can be underplayed, turned too far down, as in remaining silent and passive when a long-existing process has grown sluggish and is no longer effective. Context answers where leadership is happening and what the rules are in that particular space. As you traverse your career journey in search of next-level opportunities, know that the *theys* are watching to see if you can adjust your equalizer so that your best self can emerge and serve the unique situation at hand.

Strategic Reflection No. 13

Identify three situations typical of your world where a single leadership behavior would have a positive outcome when applied appropriately, as well as negative outcomes if applied too much and too little.

_____

_____

_____

_____

Object and Impact

Leadership is about causing a positive impact. The object that is most served by your leadership's impact is part of what defines context and what is appropriate given the situation. Leadership that is intended to affect a group of employees will walk, talk, look, and sound differently than leadership that is designed and deployed to affect a system or process. The object describes what and who is served by what your leadership efforts can offer. Although all a leader's positive efforts ultimately serve the organization in some form, context describes the most direct and immediate beneficiaries of leadership's impact. These beneficiaries are self, others, and business.

You are *leading self* when your leadership efforts positively impact or serve you and just a few others in the immediate area. You are *leading others* when your leadership efforts positively impact or help masses of people: a team, a department, or the organizational community. You are *leading business* when your leadership efforts have a positive impact *in* the business (i.e., when your leadership affects internal enterprise systems, procedures, policy, processes, or workflow) or when your leadership efforts have a positive effect *on* the business (i.e., when your leadership affects the organization's mission, vision, culture, brand, strategic priorities, or business objectives and outcomes). As you move from leading self to leading others to leading business, the area of impact expands, as does the required degree of visible competency (see figure 3). The competencies one might use to lead self will not be sufficient to lead business. When it comes to the subjects of our case studies, who or what was the primary beneficiary of each one's leadership efforts?

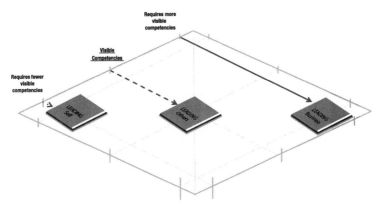

Fig. 3. The Degree of Required Competence from Leading Self to Leading Others to Leading Business

Case Study:
Petra, Trey, Jacob, and Kat

As market-development director, Petra's leadership impacted the market-development strategy. The beneficiaries of her leadership work were the business and others. Senior project manager Trey, led a team that would change how the IT department used technology to collaborate, which had broad and downstream benefits for the entire enterprise. The outcome of his work affected the business and others. As a client specialist in customer service, Jacob's leadership changed the customer experience for one longtime client of the firm, as well as the experience he was having on the job. The beneficiaries of his leadership work were others and self. As a finance analyst, Kat's leadership caused change in a way that improved how she and her team worked together to get things done, while also improving her standing as a trusted, go-to person on the team. The beneficiaries of her leadership work were others and self.

Strategic Reflection No. 14

First, what currently is the object of your leadership most of the time? Who or what benefits most directly from what your leadership has to offer? Now, think of a time when your leadership supported a different or additional object. Because you were impacting a different object, what adjustments did you make to your "equalizer" to lead effectively in this unique situation? When you think about the next-level role you want, what object will you most often impact then? In what ways might you need to broaden your use of visible leadership competencies to do so? When you think about the next-level role you want, to what extent do you need to *up* your competency game to meet its contextual demands?

_____

_____

_____

_____

_____

While Some Things Change, Some Stay the Same

In the examples in the previous case study, although the impacted objects shifted, note that the leaders' movement through the sequence remained the same. Petra, the director of market development, managed her passionate personality to successfully engage and influence her team and the conservative executive decision makers. That versatility enabled her to cause change and value in ways that impacted the business and the broader community. To cause change and value, Kat, the analyst in finance, managed her interpersonal approach to engage and influence her peers. That versatility lubricated the relationships and the flow of work, in addition to repairing her reputation in the group as someone they could trust. No matter the object, be it you, a client, the team, or the enterprise, leadership is leadership is leadership. As a leader, your job is to cause change and add value with and through others, whom you can influence, no matter their diverse needs and preferences, because you are self-mastered. As a leader, no matter the object of your leadership's impact, the sequence remains unchanged (see figure 4).

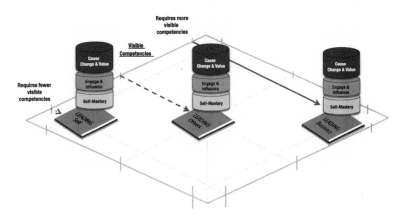

Fig. 4. Contexts Shift while the Leadership Sequence Remains Fixed

Thanksgiving Pants

Although the sequence is fixed, what does change is the demonstration and calibration of visible competency behaviors as required by the situation or context at hand. The competencies Petra leveraged and the degree to which she used them in her situation, are not the same collection and degree executed by Kat. Like an equalizer deck, Petra and Kat have to calibrate not only which visible competency behaviors can help them actualize their goals, but also *how* each one of those competencies is used. For example, to execute on Petra's goal of launching new business sites in underserved neighborhoods, she likely employed the following business-value competency behaviors:

- *Study trends and the future business landscape, while interpreting the implications.* Petra looked at the sales potential and viability of the new market.

- *Help key stakeholders respond strategically to what you have observed or recommended.* Petra delivered her findings and recommendations to the executive decision-making body with a specifically designed business case they would find compelling.

- *Create wins, advantages, or solutions for customers and other stakeholders.* Petra's plan would expand the footprint of the organization and provide the neighborhood with services it didn't currently have.

- *Help people transition to the new normal.* Part of

Petra's plan was deploying a readiness strategy across the enterprise to create a seamless transition for the organization's new clients.

Meanwhile, to move on her goal of strengthening her relationships, Kat would need to:

- *Continuously drive for results.* Even when it was painful and awkward, Kat focused on the fact that the changes she was making would advance what her team could achieve, as well as what she wanted to achieve.

- *Help people transition to the new normal.* Kat knew only time and consistency would demonstrate that her commitment to healthier relationships was sticking and authentic.

- *Learn and course correct as new data emerges.* Along the way, Kat made mistakes, learned, and refined how she related interpersonally across the team.

- *Continuously seek and pursue creative ways to innovate.* Inspiration wasn't enough to make the changes Kat wanted. She needed new skills, so Kat took classes on emotional intelligence and communication to better self-manage how she came across to others.

To execute on different goals from situation to situation—and certainly from role to role, you cannot employ the same visible competencies in a single-minded fashion. You must be situationally versatile, prioritizing the appropriate slate of visible competency behaviors to meet the demands of the circumstances you are in. The required set of visible competencies in your current role will likely be very different than the set required of you in the role you want.

However, that's not where the calibration will end. Both Petra and Kat utilized the visible competency behavior of *helping people transition to the new normal*. Given their unique situations, did they employ this particular behavior in the same way or to the same degree? In Petra's case, she had to evangelize and acclimate not only the people in the enterprise, but also the stakeholders in and around the neighborhood where the new business sites would be located. Meanwhile, in Kat's situation, applying Petra's degree of that competency behavior would have been inappropriate. Kat's situation, although it had business implications, primarily involved an interpersonal rift between Kat and her peers. Transitioning her peers to the new normal would only entail Kat being deliberate and consistent, reassuring her coworkers that the changes she committed to making were not just a temporary guise to get her out of the doghouse.

All of the competency behaviors can take on a range of forms. They all have lower-order and higher-order forms—simple and complex ways they can be delivered. In a single role, you will need to be able to demonstrate that range. In moving from one role to a next-level role, you will need to be able to demonstrate that range. Like your grandpa's Thanksgiving pants, competencies have an adjustable waistband; they expand and contract to serve the situation or the role in question. Both Petra and Kat used some of the same competencies, but their unique circumstances and their unique roles dictated that they use them very differently. That is situational versatility.

Strategic Reflection No. 15

You and your manager likely use some of the same competency behaviors to do the work of your department. Identify one behavior you share. How does your manager use that behavior in a way that is similar to you? How do you use the same competency differently? Next, think about the role you want versus the role you have. What visible competencies do the roles share? Which visible competencies are unique? Note how the same competency is used differently in your current role versus in your next. What skills do you need to develop to be able to walk in the competency behavior in its higher-order form?

Why Context Matters

Consider "Goldilocks and the Three Bears." You remember it: the story of the little girl who commandeered, by breaking and entering (a felony), the peaceful abode of an unsuspecting family of bears. Fast-forward to Goldilocks's keen examination of their chairs. One was too big; the other was too small. But finally, she came across the one that was just right. Some people, with thoughts of promotions dancing in their heads, get in their own way—and in hot water—by trying to impact an object that is way too big and far beyond their boundaries. Although they want the title and authority of leading in an enterprise-affecting role, their lower-order leading-self level of visible competency can't support it. Their competencies can't meet the needs of the situation. For other people, it's a different problem. For other people, failure comes as a result of playing it too small and too safe. Despite having the ability to play at a broader level of leadership, some lack the poise and confidence or self-mastery required to operate outside their comfort zone.

> ### An Insider Tip
> ### Develop Your Nose
>
> *Highly effective leaders have a nose or discernment for subtle changes in the environmental context that signal their need to respond accordingly. This sensitivity is something you can develop over time just by paying attention.*

As you move through your day at work, practice identifying the object that is most impacted by the demonstration of your leadership competencies in that particular context. Is it you? Does leading mean managing yourself more effectively? Is it others? Does leading mean achieving with and through the work produced by the group? Or maybe it is the business, meaning your leadership walk and talk will cause change and value in the mechanics of the work or in the tangible and nontangible results the work generates. Perhaps your leadership will positively impact all of these.

As you develop the muscle of recognizing and differentiating contexts, begin paying attention to what mix of visible leadership competency behaviors is most relevant at the time. Consider the fifty-plus leadership behaviors we have studied, and ask, in the specific situation you are in, which three to five behaviors should you prioritize? Then, as you approach a different situation, think again: Will the same three to five behaviors help you move toward a successful outcome? Maybe you just need to "turn up" the same behaviors to their higher-order forms. Or maybe you need to employ an entirely different slate of behaviors. Contrast this level of strategic thought and self-mastery with going into a situation—next level or not—asleep, feral, or out of blind habit. The

> *difference you see is part of what distinguishes a leader from others. The difference you see is self-mastery in action. The difference you see is leadership versatility.*

Although the leadership sequence is fixed, each segment of it requires more visible competencies than the last. The contextual objects of leading self, others, and business operate in the same way; each ups the ante of competencies needed from one to the next. How your leadership shows up must match the size and expectations of the context at hand. When the object of your leadership is the enterprise, it will call for a different set and different degrees of visible leadership competencies than when the object of your leadership is you or a few others in the immediate area. Your competencies, in connection with the object your leadership effects, can't be too big or too small; they must match in ways that are just right.

Strategic Reflection No. 16

Think about the next-level role you want and the visible competencies you need to demonstrate to be successful in it. Use the following table to organize your thoughts. In the first column, "Competency Behavior," list three competency behaviors you will need to demonstrate in the next-level role. In the second column, "Well Played," for each competency you noted, describe what the competency would look like when appropriately executed. Next, in the third column, "Over- or

Underplayed," describe the same competency, but this time, as demonstrated by someone playing it too big or too small. How would the same competency look if displayed by someone who was not ready to take on the next-level role? How would it look if exhibited by someone who wasn't using his or her full potential? Finally, think about how you normally walk in the competency. Are you closer to well played or over- or underplayed? What do you need to learn or demonstrate to close the gap?

A Competency Behavior Found in the Next-Level Role	Well Played in the Next-Level Role	Over- or Underplayed in the Next-Level Role

_____

_____

_____

_____

_____

_____

Climbing the Stairs

Sometimes shifts in context are difficult to discern; other times, they are obvious. In the average organization, there are standard elevations of leadership, or hierarchies. These hierarchical contexts dictate how much formally sanctioned power a leader wields, the salary the leader earns, and the scope of a leader's measurable accountabilities. But hierarchies also dictate elevations of expected behavior. Often, those expectations are not straightforward and easy to discern. They are nuanced and, at times, even contradictory.

For each level of leadership, the landscape is complicated and wrought with context conundrums. These tension points between competing forces present vulnerabilities that can make leadership contenders like you appear ill fit for the next-level roles you want. If you are not responsive to these subtle dilemmas, it can distort the perception of your leadership readiness for what's next at work. As we climb the stairs of the standard hierarchies you would likely find in an organization, think about the obvious and nuanced expectations of leaders at different levels—and moreover, how you might manage the subtler context conundrums that often test whether you should be taken seriously at the next level as leadership material.

Senior-Level Leaders

Senior-level leaders are generally the direct or second-tier reports of individuals in the most high-ranking roles of the organization—the C-suite, which is typically made up of people whose titles include "chief officer," e.g., CEO (chief executive officer), CFO (chief financial officer), and others. These chiefs have the highest-level oversight of several large functional areas in the organization. These large functions commonly include Shared Services (Human Resources, IT, and Accounting—groups all departments in the organization use), Marketing and Sales, Operations, Client Services, Philanthropy and Foundations, Research and Development as well as Production, and others—depending on the type of organization it is. Heading each of these functional areas is a senior-level leader who, along with his or her peers—the other functional owners, works under a single chief's reporting umbrella.

Although senior-level leaders—department executives, vice presidents, department heads, senior directors, and so forth—typically have a large staff of direct and indirect reports, their primary roles and accountabilities are related to the strategic performance of the organization. They are the strategists, and their core responsibilities include supporting the enterprise—now and future-looking—through the lens of the functions they manage. A senior-level leader's line of business (LOB), which includes smaller departments, divisions, teams, and staff members, contributes to or actualizes the enterprise strategy according to a set slate of high-level metrics, measurements, and goals. Relative to their people-management responsibilities, senior-level leaders are the head of a large pyramid of employees, specifically managing multiple high-level and mid level managers (e.g., vice presidents, assistant vice presidents, and directors), each of whom, in turn, manages a range of middle or frontline managers, and below these, individual contributors, and associates. A senior-level leader's job is anticipating long-range change, threats, and opportunities in the market while leveraging enterprise resources to facilitate sufficient long-term budgeting, talent, and technologies for that leader's LOB.

Leaders at this level have three parts to their roles: they are peers and partners of the other department heads beside them, they are champions of the unique priorities of their own LOBs, and they coach their LOB's coaches. Put another way, they push good management practice down into (and through) the layers of managers in their own hierarchies. With all of that comes a tangled mess of competing aims, scarcity of resources, and complicated social politics. In front of that backdrop, senior-level leaders must perform a balancing act between being, along with their peers, a collaborative co-steward of the enterprise resources, strategizing and advocating for the specific needs of their own LOBs, while also managing the people, who will manage the people, who will do the work in their area of the business.

At this level, a common context conundrum rises from leaders favoring one side of the role versus the others. Next to his or her peers, the other LOB owners, is the leader a collaborator or a competitor? Does the senior leader prefer strategizing the business to developing the people—or the other way around? What the *theys* will want to see is someone who can be a cooperative partner across the range of senior-level peers, an effective champion capable of winning resources for the business the leader specifically owns, as well as a committed coach to the rising next generation of managers who will one day have the reins of the LOB.

At first glance, the leadership competencies that add business value may appear to hold the answer for this conundrum. However, at this level, it is likely that leaders are delegating much of that tactical work to others in their hierarchies. Thus, their context conundrum is best met through activating leadership competencies that add relationship value. To navigate the complicated social waters at this level, leaders will need to demonstrate the ability to negotiate laterally, as well as grow the competencies in their own vertical lines of direct reports. But to build these mutually beneficial bridges beside and downward, such leaders must also have full mastery of themselves.

Strategic Reflection No. 17

Imagine you are a leader at this level. What kinds of visible competency behaviors would you employ to compete? What kinds of visible competency behaviors would you employ to cooperate? What kinds of visible competency behaviors would you employ to coach? What would you need to do to be effective at all three simultaneously?

_____

_____

_____

_____

_____

_____

_____

_____

The Middle-Level Leader

Leaders at this level (e.g., directors, front-line managers, supervisors) are typically people managers who have responsibility for driving the directives that come from above. They receive their goals from the senior-management level and translate those objectives into plans that will be executed by the teams and people the middle-level leader manages day to day. The middle-level leader's role is to act as an enabler. Positioned between the strategists and the people who actually perform the work, the middle-level leader's job is to identify, engage, coach, develop, and drive talent and results so that the LOB can deliver its contribution to the organization's health and well-being. Whereas the senior-level leaders facilitate global support, the middle-level leaders deploy and allocate local support toward the talent, budget, and technology needs of the teams.

This level of leader has to simultaneously manage a number of equally powerful drivers of business results: people, production, and plans—as well as a tempting shortcut. Their responsibility is to enable people to produce by driving the plan. The evidence of successfully juggling this trinity requires delegating to and influencing employees to perform. However, there is a tempting alternative: underdelegating or just doing it themselves.

At this level, the context conundrum emerges from a leader engaging in tactics as a doer, thereby obscuring and diminishing the leader's presence as an enabler. The *theys* will want to see leaders who develop, empower, and engage the full strength of their teams. Although these leaders are still often seen as producing, they should be increasingly seen as doing so through their employees' hands.

Another vulnerability rises from middle-level leaders living between two worlds: the strategic world above them and the tactical one below. Commonly, these leaders rose from the ranks of the tactical world as an associate. Thus, it can be tempting, especially for new or emerging leaders at this level, to fall back into the tasks, assignments, and the *doing* that proved them management-worthy in the first place. But in this new role of *managing* those that *do*, a leader must deliver through the collective work of a group. When people managers overly engage in tactics, they are underutilizing their most important asset, their people, as well as their second most important asset, themselves as individuals who manage the collective work of many.

Some leaders at this level fall the other way. They wholeheartedly embrace moving out of tactics and quickly bed a nest in strategic work. That choice, also, can prove a fatal mistake. Teams need care and feeding. They need support and coaching. Neglecting to manage the people means the middle-level leader is depriving their teams of the relational and developmental oxygen they need to thrive.

Here, all three categories of competencies are useful. Understanding the business helps leaders at this level value the strategic viewpoint driving the goals that descend from above. It also helps the enablers set the framework for plans and results, as well as serve as an effective agent of change. But effectiveness in these types of roles also requires relationship building. Smack dab in the middle of everything, these leaders must influence up, down, and sideways. That will take immense self-mastery and versatility to move agilely between those altitudes and each one's very distinctive needs.

Strategic Reflection No. 18

Most roles have a tactical (doing) side and a strategic (thinking and planning) side. Which part of your role do you enjoy most? How would you manage it if the next-level role you want pulls you away from the tactical or strategic work you enjoy?

_____

_____

_____

_____

_____

_____

_____

_____

_____

Senior-Level Nonmanaging Specialists and Professionals

There is another set of often-unsung senior leaders: senior-level subject matter experts (SMEs), and can include in-house accountants, auditors, attorneys, and consultants. Instead of people management, these senior specialists and professionals contribute specialized knowledge, as well as a deep and broad understanding of concepts, ideas, and next and best practices. They are typically deployed to reduce risks and business threats or, through their unique skill-sets, help meet the business' imperatives and goals. They, too, are enablers, commonly used as internal advisors to executive, senior- and middle-level managers.

These leaders have the unique responsibility of influencing without the power of direct authority. Instead, they use their knowledge as currency to position themselves as specialized problem solvers, which in itself creates a challenge. For most effective SMEs, their expertise rises from a deep passion and curiosity about the subject matter. SMEs know their stuff better than anyone else, down to the atomic level. Although this depth of knowledge can be a blessing, it can also be their curse.

Leaders of this type have often made a large personal and financial investment in their specialized education, licensure, and certification that evidence their love of their specialty. Ironically, it is that same love that can set them up to fall into the context conundrum and misconception that their internal clients need or want the same level of detail the SME enjoys. SMEs often struggle to edit themselves, displaying an inability to discern the line between all they know about a subject and the amount of data their internal clients need to make a decision. What the *theys* will want to see is someone who can keep it simple, elegant, and laser focused on the problem that the internal clients want the SME, through his or her deep knowledge, to solve. The *theys* want someone who, on the one hand, can understand the depth of the subject like a scientist yet, on the other hand, can boil it down like a bourbon that's smooth and well distilled for the layperson to imbibe.

SMEs already leverage business competencies through the lens of their beloved area of interest. However, SMEs must self-manage their detailed technical passion and artfully translate their deep knowledge for laypeople who share neither the specialized expertise nor the SMEs passion, and only want a clear recommendation they can understand and act on. To do this, SMEs will also have to activate their relationship competencies almost as much as they do their unique know-how.

Strategic Reflection No. 19

Think about a subject area that deeply interests you and on which you are often called upon to advise or consult at work. In the space provided, list sixteen data points you know about that topic.

1.	9.
2.	10.
3.	11.
4.	12.
5.	13.
6.	14.
7.	15.
8.	16.

Next, think about each item relative to how critical it is in helping one of your internal clients solve an urgent problem. With that in mind, give each item one of the following labels: necessary to know (NTK) or interesting to know (ITK). Lastly, if you had to reduce the list down to the most important points for informing your internal client's decision, which three items would you keep? Circle these items. This is the kind of strategy you may have to use to reduce and laser focus large amounts of complex information that interests you as a SME, but may overwhelm your audience of laypeople.

Individual Contributors and Associates

Individual contributors and associates directly engage with the organization's products, processes, and projects, and through that interaction, they cause positive change relative to business objectives. These are the doers, the leaders who are often thought of or challenged as not being in leadership at all. Some point to the limited formal power and influence of these individual contributors and associates as evidence that this group is not really composed of leaders. And yet they must follow the same sequence all leaders do: self-mastery, engaging and influencing circumstance and people, and causing change and value.

Individual contributors and associates are vulnerable to the name game of being individuals who walk and talk like a leader long before the *theys* will formally call them one. This is their context conundrum. What the *theys* want to see is results, specifically, someone who gets them as a leader does: by self-mastering and influencing others. The results—and the leader-like way in which the results are achieved—must become so closely linked with the person that the *theys* cannot think of one without the other.

Individual contributors and associates must deal with the semantics and powerful word web in which they often find themselves caught. The argument is that because they do not hold the title of supervisor, team lead, manager, senior manager, or director, they are not leaders. Although I wholly disagree, in the real world, associates will have to wait and self-manage their frustration and patience as they look for ways to get positive visibility. "Manager" is not a title they possess, but leadership is a state one chooses to own and walk in. Individual contributors' efforts to cause change and add value or influence people and circumstances may go unnoticed and unrewarded for a long time. Their growing leadership capability may attract uncompensated work that offers little more than an informal audition to demonstrate what they can do. But these leaders must stay the course. Patience is part of the journey, testing the strength of what they want and their willingness to wait and work for it.

Strategic Reflection No. 20

Regardless of your current leadership level, you are likely fulfilling one of four functions in your current role in the organization: doer, SME enabler, managing enabler, or strategist. Which function best describes where you are in your organization? When you think about the context conundrums present in each role, what can you do to manage these vulnerabilities that can diminish your evident readiness for your next-level goals?

_____

_____

_____

_____

_____

Getting Started

Think about your goals, such as a promotion, or the next-level role you want. Do your current competencies match the level of impact expected in the position you desire? You may be accustomed to operating in the contexts of leading self and leading others, for example. But the promotion you want is at the level of leading business. Which behaviors will you need to develop to improve your readiness for what's next at work? What will you need to do or stop doing to position yourself as suitable? Or perhaps it's not about acquiring new behaviors but using the ones you already have differently.

If you are feeling the sensation of déjà vu, you're not crazy; you're right on track. This habit of reflecting, based on your self-awareness, and then selecting the most appropriate approach given the situation at hand is at the heart of self-mastery. Although it is one of the most essential components and thus was introduced early on, even at these advanced stages of your strategy to manifest evident leadership, you will need self-mastery more than ever. That's because to be a leader, what you do has to be done not only *with purpose* but also *on purpose.*

Chapter 9

LEADERSHIP COMMERCE

The economics of leadership brand

LET'S TALK BLING and burgers. Tiffany & Co. is associated with pale-blue boxes, elegant white bows, and diamonds. McDonald's is associated with hamburgers, Happy Meals, golden fries, and golden arches. Branding is the linking of a thing to a belief or feeling, to the extent that one cannot be imagined without the other. When most hear Tiffany, they think bling. When most see a McDonald's, they think burgers. However, a brand does more than that. When romance calls, many think of Tiffany & Co. diamonds and happily serve up 4 months salary. When hunger on the run pangs, the golden arches spell fast, cheap, and tasty relief—and out comes $5.99. Companies hope the action their brand evokes is consumers buying what they are selling. Branding does more than link and conjure association; it converts thought into action. Brand association compels more than linking two things together. Brand association compels consumers to do something as a result.

Top Shelf

You are a product. You are a human resource to your organization. From you, your organization buys your time, talent, energy, and effort. You have consumers. They are the people and groups that consume or use what you offer. If you are a manager, one group of consumers is your employees, who use your direction, your feedback, and the systems you have put in place to help them do their jobs. Likewise, your boss is also a consumer; your boss uses the combined work and value your team creates. Even if you are an individual contributor, again, you can count your boss among your consumers, along with the individuals and groups with whom you work. It does not matter whether these are external customers or people who work a few cubicles away. If their problems are solved or if their needs are met through you, they are your consumers. If they use the deliverables you produce, you are a product. And like all products you have a brand.

Your brand is your reputation—what people say when you're not in the room, your unique and signature offerings and contributions that others associate with you, and what you are known for in the organization. Even at this very moment, right now, as you read these words, congratulations—you have a bouncing baby brand. Whether you knew it already or not, and like it or not, you have a brand. Not only do you have a brand, but it's a strong one and not easily changed. Whether you have a brand is not and was never the question. The question is and was always: What is your brand? And more importantly, is it one that will serve your goal of being seen as ready for the next level?

Answering that question will depend on what your consumers, and the *theys* among them, associate with you. When the *theys* see your face, hear your name, or think about you, do they think leadership? Your leadership brand is the association the *theys* have made between you and your ability to create positive change and add value in the organization. That association is based on the consistent way as well as the extent to which others experience your leadership value. Brands, remember, are intended to do more than just link a thing and a thought together; they also compel an action. Your leadership brand drives how others respond to you. That response could include others respecting, admiring, and following you. And conversely, that response could consist of others avoiding you, passing you over, or not noticing your leadership capabilities at all. Perception is reality. If the *theys* look at you and link you and leadership, you are one—and the way they react to you will back that up. If they look at you and don't link you and leadership, you aren't—and the way they react to you will back that up too.

Sticky lil' Beasts

Years ago, there was a popular movie called *Gremlins,* which centered on these cute and cuddly creatures who held a mysterious and destructive little secret. And if their handlers wanted to avoid all hell breaking loose, they needed to follow a serious set of rules, caveats, and parameters. Brands are similar little beasts. Brands are complex, powerful, necessary things that can grow, flourish, and under the right conditions, accelerate your success story at work. But, if handled the wrong way, they can create as much damage as they can good.

For starters, a brand, with the right care and feeding, is an efficient and powerful endorsement. It can be your calling card, establishing your credibility even before you have entered the space. But, brands do have limitations. Your desired brand, what you want to be, or what you claim to be, cannot compete with others' actual experience with you. People will believe what they experience, not what you tell them, making self-mastery, once again, a critical component of your leadership success strategy. Back in the win column is the fact that your positive brand is strong, deeply rooted, and difficult to change, but it is not impervious. It can suffer damage—and that damage can have real-world consequences. Damaging a brand can be effortless, even accidental—and that damage, once in place, is as sticky as glue—but luckily it isn't necessarily a life sentence. And once again, we encounter the value of causing value. Delivering value in your organization can give your brand the toughness it needs to endure trials and tribulations—even those you inflict on yourself. Even in the face of your own errors and folly, if you create enough value, people will forgive, overlook it, and hold their noses.

An Insider Tip
The "F" word

Your brand is yours, and it's not yours. No matter how you would like your brand to be defined, in many ways, it's not up to you, and at the same time, it is. Others largely define your brand based on how they consistently experience you. That's the part that belongs to others. But the onus to change, strengthen, and sustain your positive brand is on you. So the first step to managing your brand is figuring out the current state of what it is.

The most direct way to accomplish this is to ask for feedback. You can go the formal route by using a 360-degree assessment instrument that invites others to give you their perceptions, which you, in turn, can compare and contrast with your own. But there are less formal ways as well. Generate a list of words and phrases—both positive and negative—that describe robust and weak leadership. Then ask a small group of people to indicate which ones they associate with you. An even less formal way is to ask your most trusted friends what they hear associated with you in and around the job. However, the easiest way is to listen to the feedback you're likely already getting from your manager and consumers on how you perform. However you choose to take your reputational temperature, be warned.

You may not like all that you learn. That is to be expected. At this stage, managing your brand is not about perfection; it's about diagnosis. Take a deep breath and remain open. Everything you hear you can likely change with the right know-how. Getting defensive, in the face of critical feedback, is a fast way to show professional immaturity. Plain and simple—you accomplish *nothing but demonstrating why you're not yet fit to lead.*

When it comes to positive feedback, don't take it and run. Stop and dissect it. You achieved a positive result—but why? What did you do or avoid doing that caused the right outcome? Whatever behaviors rest behind that why are the gems you need to get at and dig out. Learn what they are, and all that you have to do to win again is wash 'n repeat.

Also, getting no data is getting data. If nothing positive or negative is associated with you, or if people are reluctant to give you information, that, in itself, is information. Perhaps, your value-add isn't visible—or it is, but people don't want to tell you what they see. And just like Kat's manager cautioned, if you invite the truth and people give it to you, don't punish them for doing what you asked.

What nonleaders do, in the face of feedback they don't like, is get pouty or complacent. What leaders do, in the face of feedback, is get busy. If the feedback you receive disappoints you, it is only a signal that there is more work to be done. And even if it doesn't, there is still work to do. And if you are really a leader, you will quickly get about the business of doing it.

Brand By Design

What is the "it" you have to do to reinvent your brand or re-create it with intention? You must do what commodities like Tiffany & Co. and McDonald's do—make a promise. Their brands make a promise relative to what they will consistently deliver. Their brands say what you can consistently and uniquely expect from them. Tiffany promises to deliver romance embodied in a diamond. McDonald's promises to deliver easy, fast, and tasty burgers. What do you promise, through your leadership, to uniquely deliver? What do you offer that is unlike what others can? Chapters ago, in upgrading your introduction, you approached it. Now it's time to go all in. And to do so, we first have to go where value resides. I'm not talking about the apartment on Twentieth Street, two blocks down from the corner bodega. When it comes to how you uniquely add value, I'm talking about going where value unexpectedly lives.

Value lives in pain. Value lives in gaps. Value lives in problems. Value lives in your consumers' problems that you swoop in to solve with your time, talent, energy, and effort. Value also lives in advantage. Value lives in the additional benefits your consumers gain when your time, talent, energy, and effort deliver. After many years of getting experience, making mistakes, receiving great mentoring, and completing rigorous training, *my* value, for example, lives in my ability to offer coaching, support, and insight to those who want to lead or lead more effectively. But where's the pain? Where's the gap? If value lives in pain, where is it?

Many people are fortunate to have generous mentoring and nurturing managers who are prepared to invest in their professional growth. And then there are those who must make their own luck. In one role I had in corporate human resources, my job was brokering leadership development for high potentials and emerging senior leaders. It was such fun work—very entrepreneurial, as our group, focused particularly on leadership development, was brand spanking new. My job was aligning employees, whose talent had been identified by their business units, with expensive coaches and other formal development opportunities. And their lines of business (LOB) would sponsor it. A few years passed and we, in the team, were happy to see that leadership development in the organization had seemingly normalized. One day, I pulled data on how deeply our leadership development work was penetrating. How many employees did the work really touch? What I found shocked me, and looking back, likely changed my life forever.

Of the eligible leaders who could receive formal leadership development beyond the average management training class, only about 3% ever did. In an organization that had about 9,000 people working at various levels of management, about 8,730 would not receive formal leadership development. There were reasons—none of them satisfying. Maybe we, in the group, hadn't sufficiently evangelized the virtues of leadership development throughout the organization. The LOBs, with their strict budgets, could only sponsor so many. Many thought, a manager spending time in a development program was a manager who was not on the floor doing the job. And in some areas of the organization, formal development just wasn't a priority. These managers were smart people, the rationale argued. They would figure it out for themselves.

Wow! I remember eyeing the analytics that said thousands of worthy people would have to manufacture and cobble a path towards success all on their own. When I left corporate to work for myself, to that particular pain, I aimed to offer a salve. Part of the value I hope to provide is giving these worthy people what they may not otherwise have: professional partnership, access to leadership acumen, strategic insight, and confidence. My value rises from the problems I can help my clients solve and from the advantages I can help them attain more expeditiously. Where does *your* value live? Whose pain do you help relieve? From what problems or yet-unrealized advantages does your value-add arise?

Strategic Reflection No. 21

Earlier, you learned how to upgrade your introduction by describing what you help people do. Designing your unique leadership brand statement takes that a step further. Start with your consumers. Who are they? What is it that they want to achieve? Next, describe what additional advantage is captured *and* what pain or disadvantage is avoided when you deliver. Here's the formula.

I help (*who*) do (*a desired outcome*), so that they can have (*benefit/value*) without (*disadvantage/pain*).

For example, here's what I would write: "I help professionals and managers (*who*) develop their leader-craft so they can drive great results with and through their people (*a desired outcome*) with confidence and competence (*captured advantage or value*) instead of the doubt, stress, and insecurity of going it alone (*avoided disadvantage or pain*)." I showed you my brand statement; now show me yours.

_____

_____

_____

_____

_____

_____

_____

Your leadership brand is your stated promise to solve a problem, accelerate an advantage, and deliver value in your unique way. Like McDonald's, you are promising to deliver fast and uniform burgers when someone is hungry and in a hurry. Like Tiffany & Co., you have promised to deliver stunning elegance expressed in a clear and colorless diamond. Like powerful commodities, the most effective leaders decide for themselves who and what they want to be to the people around them. What salve do you promise to deliver?—to soothe what pain? —and for whom? But even when those answers crystalize, promising to deliver is the easy part; now you have to deliver, now you have to *do* leadership—and in ways that solidify, grow, and sustain your leadership reputation.

Brand Strategy 1: To Keep It,
You Must Give It Away

The gifts, strengths, or talents that you uniquely offer are not finite in supply. Every time you exercise them, they do not diminish. They flourish. They multiply. In fact, the fastest way to lose your strengths is to keep them under wraps. Especially if you intend to build your brand as leadership material, you must do the opposite and with vigor. At every opportunity, you must use your gifts to help others solve problems or accelerate their contact with an advantage. Unlike water in a glass that is reduced with consumption, your strengths are more like muscles that only grow with use.

To establish your link with highly competent, highly effective, and highly reliable leadership, you must demonstrate competence, effectiveness, and reliability every chance you get. You must look for opportunities—not to show off but to just do what you do. I saw a meme once that said: "The lion is most beautiful when he hunts." I took it to mean that we are at our best when we do what we are designed to do. Do what you were designed to do. Do it often. Do it without fail. Do it until it is what you are known for.

Brand Strategy 2: Apply Newton's Third Law

You learned it in grade school: Isaac Newton's third law, which states that every action yields an equal and opposite reaction. Newton's law taught us about cause and effect and that everything we do, including our mishaps or inaction, causes a result. Brands can be altered. They can be damaged—even on accident. But if that is true, it means they can also be improved—on purpose. Now next to that, lay this quote by American poet and civil rights activist Maya Angelou: "I've learned people will forget what you said, people will forget what you did, but people will never forget how you made them feel."

How do you want the *theys* in your organization to feel as a result of working with you? When your consumers leave your presence, what do you want them to think? When you're not in the room, what feelings should the mention of your name evoke? Old Isaac would likely suggest the following: decide what you want others to think and feel about you, then determine which of your consistent behaviors will cause it.

For example, an internal consultant in your organization might say, "I want my consumers, when they leave my presence, to feel like they've received sound advice they can trust." Now the question becomes: What does this internal consultant need to do, say, avoid doing, and avoid saying to cause people to trust her word, advice, and counsel when she gives it? What does she need to do to deliver on her desired leadership brand? The answer to this consultant's question would include making sure her opinions are well researched and studied, taking opportunities to speak or become a known thought leader on a particular topic within the organization, and consistently guiding her consumers toward solid answers in a way that keeps the consumers' confidence intact. What would all those deliberate actions yield? What would a consumer who consistently experienced the positive results of those choices likely think about the professional who delivered them? I think it's reasonable and likely that this leader will have earned the brand she wanted. Now it's your turn.

Strategic Reflection No. 22

Think about what you promised to deliver through your Brand Statement in Strategic Reflection No. 21. Now think about an average day at work. Think about the choices you make throughout the day. What big ones are you making? What small ones are you making? To whom do you talk or neglect to talk around your office? What do you say or fail to say? Now ask: Do the choices you make, both big and small, cause the unique leadership brand you want? Do they deliver what you promise through your brand? Now that you have decided who and what you are going to be by designing a leadership brand statement, what do you need to stop doing, start doing, and continue doing to become what your brand statement says you are?

_____

_____

_____

_____

_____

_____

_____

Brand Strategy 3: Know What You Can Afford

Within your lifetime, you have probably had the misfortune of encountering a phony or disingenuous person. Sadly, most of us have. Although we probably didn't know the person very well, why and how did we determine that he or she was not to be trusted? What was it about that person that reeked of dishonesty and told our instincts to be suspicious? Perhaps the word itself can give us clues. According to the *Merriam-Webster* dictionary, the word *phony* developed from the British term *fawney*, which described the gilded brass rings that were used as the hook in a con game called the *fawney rig*.[20]

The trick involved a grifter getting the grifted to pay for something that appeared real and valuable but was actually fake. Like this fool's gold, a phony person instigates a conflict between what's real and what's not. A phony person doesn't walk around with "phony" written on his or her forehead to forewarn us. Rather, it's something we can faintly sense. We can't put a finger on it, but it's there. Maybe somewhere in our subconscious, we can see the fighting between what the phony person claims to be and what he or she actually is.

Is the leader you claim to be fighting with what you actually do? Critical to the delicate work of managing what other people believe about you is consistency. You are what you most often do. Leaders choose to do things that nonleaders don't. To be seen as a leader, you must decide to do and say things that support what you want people to see, which is that you are an effective leader and worthy of climbing to the next level at work.

However, sooner or later (probably sooner), even when you have diligently built your leadership brand in the mind of the *theys*, you will encounter situations that will test your commitment to the brand you've worked so hard to construct. Sooner or later, you will have to choose between something that aligns with, and is contrary to, your leadership brand. Because it is circumstance that makes a behavior appropriate or not, this dilemma is resolved by weighing the "economy of choice," which is a simple concept that reminds us about the balance of rewards and consequence inherent in any move we make. It reminds us that when we choose one thing as a leader, we are rejecting something else. Put another way, every behavior you choose or don't choose buys something, costs something, and you must know whether, as a leader, you can afford to pay.

Case Study: Trey, Senior Project Manager and Subject-Matter Expert, Information Technology

When we last saw Trey, he had successfully led a cross-functional team and created change with broad positive impacts across the organization. But there's been a new development. Trey's manager and his manager's manager have taken notice, and they told him so. After several minutes of high praise, Trey's boss and his boss' boss left him with this thought: "Keep up this level of success and we may need to make a manager of you." And it wasn't just talk. In the weeks that *followed, discussion about developing Trey for a formal leadership role seemed to make its way into more of the one-on-ones he had with his boss. Trey had never considered it, not until now. Now, Trey finds himself asking it too... the same tantalizing question the theys are: If Trey could achieve this much with no authority, what could he do with it?*

Trey knows that pursuing this opportunity, like all choices, won't be free. If Trey wants to build his brand and the theys' confidence that he is ready to take the wheel, he can't just be successful this one time; he needs to do it repeatedly. Success has to become his normal and become associated with his name. The angel on Trey's shoulder sees the virtue in the suggestion. Repeating his success would make his ability undeniable, dramatically improving his chances of being seen as ready for the next step at work. But the devil on Trey's other shoulder has a problem. Why in the world would Trey keep acting like a people manager, doing the work of one, taking the risk of one, when he's not getting paid like one?

It's a fair question, and there are many ways Trey can respond to this opportunity. As the devil on his shoulder whispers on, Trey may react with fear of the unknown or with resentment for being asked to deliver first and be promoted second. However, if he applies the economy of choice, Trey can make his decision based on the brand he wants to build, and not just on the voices emanating from his shoulders. To do that, Trey needs to consider the following:

- *What does repeating his success as a project manager buy?* It creates example after example, proof on top of proof that Trey can succeed, even without authority.

- *However, what does the same action cost?* It costs time, energy, and the risk of doing the job well before Trey gets the perks, power, and compensation that go along with it.

- *Can his brand afford it?* That will depend on the strength of Trey's goal of making his leadership capability evident to the *theys* around him.

Whatever Trey decides, in using the economy of choice, Trey is already demonstrating leadership of self because he is choosing based on having counted the costs and rewards. He's making a choice with intention. That's what leaders do. And personally, I hope Trey chooses to *afford* the opportunity presented to him.

But what about Jacob and *his* brand dilemma? Like Trey, Jacob, the client specialist in customer service, also wants to be seen as leadership material, and he has worked diligently to build his reputation as a calm, levelheaded, helpful pro in what can be a very stressful customer service environment. Imagine Jacob listening to his irate customer, on her third or fourth round of blaming him for her confusion.

Now, press the pause button.
Everything freezes in place.

In that moment, Jacob has to do the math, weighing what his choices buy and cost. Giving his customer the tongue-lashing she deserves: What would it "buy" him? Satisfaction, the release of tension, and giving her what she has coming to her! But what does snapping back at her cost? His reputation that he's worked hard to build. This cost, given his goal, is it something Jacob can afford? Is it something he *wants* to afford?

Just for fun, let's take Jacob out of his customer service chair and put him smack dab in the middle of a burning building. Next to him, inside the inferno, is someone who, instead of escaping the flames with his life, would rather sit and see how the cliffhanger on his favorite binge series ends. Most of us would agree that Jacob snapping, even screaming, at this person to help him grasp the gravity of the situation would be a reasonable choice. In that instance, Jacob's leadership brand can afford the bruised ego of the person he's rescuing from certain death. But back in his chair in the customer service department, snapping at his customer is something Jacob can't afford, not if he wants what he wants, and that's to be seen as a leader. Like Trey, I hope Jacob chooses wisely. To walk and talk in the leadership brand you want, I hope you do too.

Strategic Reflection No. 23

Think of a circumstance in which you behaved in a way that was contrary to your leadership brand, ultimately causing a negative outcome. What evidence indicates that your choice cost you more than you initially anticipated? If you had the decision to make over again, knowing what it would ultimately cost your brand, what would you have chosen instead?

_____

_____

_____

_____

_____

_____

_____

_____

_____

Tool or Trap

In February of 2018, the Pew Research Center reported that approximately 7 in 10 Americans use social media to connect with friends and family, for news, to share selfies and other important information, and for entertainment.[21] When it comes to social media, most of us are out there, in living-color pictures and messages, on Facebook, LinkedIn, Instagram, YouTube, Twitter, Pinterest, and countless other platforms. But for professionals focused on building their brands as highly competent leaders, social media can be a useful reinforcing tool or a trap that undermines and contradicts who and what you say you are.

If the *theys* googled you, what would they find? And would whatever they found align with the person you purport to be? Would they see content that presents you as compatible with your work's espoused philosophies? Or would they find messages and images that compromise your claim as a leader ready for the next level in your organization's particular culture? Even as I write this, I can hear some of you say: *My social media footprint is my own! I'm not on the clock! What about free speech?* Yes, in the United States, we enjoy that freedom. But no one is immune from speech or choices without consequences.

I like social media. It provides the potential for human connectivity, the likes of which we had never seen before. While it comes with challenges, risks, and trolls, social media gives us the platform to share what we are, the mix of our simplicity and our complexity—our simplexity. For me, there are those memes, images, quotes, and news stories that well represent and resonate with me as a living, breathing, thinking, and feeling woman, who is a pragmatic optimist, smarty-pants, mother, hard-working professional, and fallible human being with a sense of humor, personality, culture, and a point of view that is socially conscious and politically aware. Personally, there have been thousands of times when I shared something that gave me a good belly laugh on Facebook, only to return and adjust the privacy setting for friends only. And sometimes, it was better to delete it altogether—those things that are not for the eyes and sensibilities of those beyond my closest intimates. The determining litmus test I use is simple.

I only publically share what someone would likely learn or infer of me if we spent an afternoon together over coffee. I like plain ol' joe, by the way—no sugar, and lots of cream.

An Insider Tip
Managing Social Media

When it comes to posting on social media, determine what your litmus test is. What differentiates between what you will show the world, what is for you, or what is only for the eyes of your closest friends? Use the economy of choice to decide which messages and images are rightly or advantageously associated with you on social media—versus those things, which could potentially cost you too much. Judge between those things that humanize you versus those things that chip away at a brand that could help lift you to your next-level goals.

Gauge how sensitive your organization is to the range of the publicly espoused opinions and points of view of its employees.

Periodically google your name—all forms, including shortened, maiden, or hyphenated versions—to see for yourself what others will. From there, make adjustments as needed.

And if you are ever in doubt, just don't post it.

Nothing is free. Everything—every response, every choice, every action (whether it's taken by you or your digital avatar), buys a benefit and costs a consequence. Here, again, is the nature of polarity. Choosing a behavior means choosing the benefits and the costs that come with it while simultaneously rejecting the benefits and costs of something else. Then the economy of choice asks: "Is your choice (with its costs and benefits) something your brand can afford?"

Priorities

Think for a moment about the subjects of our case studies: Petra, the market development director; Trey, the information technology subject-matter expert; Jacob, the client specialist; and Kat, the finance analyst. Which leaders, at what levels, need to prioritize attending to their leadership brand? Because leadership is leadership is leadership, regardless of the level, the same applies to managing the perceptions about you in the organization, right? The part of me that is a teacher and wants everyone to reach their fullest potential wants to tell you that all four of the leaders we've been following should have equal concern about their reputations.

However, I'm also a realist and am committed to giving it to you straight. As one who is leading business, Petra needs to apply the most intentional energy, effort, and conscientiousness to her brand. The stage on which she is performing is broad, and the light on her—and her capability—is turned up high. If I were coaching Petra on brand management, the practices that maintain one's reputation, her leadership brand might be a priority in our development plan (see figure 5). Petra's brand management will cost her the price of having to master and apply more visible competencies. But given the exposure she has, it's worth it.

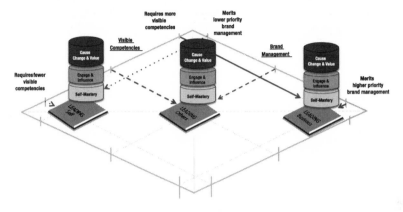

Fig. 5. Increasing Priority of Brand Management
as the Object of Impact Ascends

That doesn't let Trey, Jacob, and Kat off the hook, though—not at all. Petra is an established leader. Her test is one of ascending to a higher level relative to a ladder she is already climbing. Jacob and Kat, who are primarily leaders of self, need to prove their readiness to ascend in their careers also. They should put intentional energy, effort, and conscientiousness into their leadership brand too. However, if I were coaching them, brand management might be farther down on our list of development priorities. At this point, their stage is much smaller, and the light on them is much dimmer, at least for now. They would do better to concentrate on demonstrating higher-order forms of the leadership competencies needed in the jobs they have now as well as in the ones they want later.

Trey is the man in the middle. His reputation and brand are currencies he'll increasingly need to lead, with and without authority, and as he manages upward, downward, and sideways. Like Petra, the price he pays will be the effort it takes Trey to master more visible competencies. If I were coaching him, managing his brand might not be our first priority, but it would likely be a close second or third.

Getting Started

As you go about an average day, you make thousands of choices, starting with the first: getting your behind out of bed. Once at work, the choices continue. You choose to do things and not do them. You choose to say things and not say them. You make choices every minute of every day. What do your choices buy you? Cost you? And can you afford them? Practice asking yourself the economy of choice questions as part of your decision-making process.

Practice being present enough to recognize when you are making a choice. For example, before attending your next meeting at work, while still sitting at your desk, appreciate all the decisions you are about to make. You will choose to go or not. You will choose to be on time or not. You will choose to come prepared or not. You will choose to listen intently to the presentation and engage in the conversation or not.

I hope you go to your meeting—on time and prepared. I hope you listen and actively participate. However, just for a moment, consider the rewards and consequences of not doing those things. Not going may be easier and, depending on the meeting, much more desirable. Not showing up on time would take less effort and conscientiousness. Sitting there and thinking about your weekend plans would be much easier compared to leaning in and engaging in a business conversation.

Now consider what you want. If you are reading this, I'll assume what you want is to be seen as a leader or a higher ranking one. Then ask whether not going, not being on time, not being prepared, and not engaging, although easier and perhaps more desirable options, will buy you the brand or reputation you need to be seen as the leader you really are. Practice doing the mental calculus regarding what your choices buy and cost. Start with small decisions, then apply the process to more serious ones. Trust me, as you climb, making the right calculations will become more and more critical to your success. Being a leader is a choice, and it doesn't come cheaply. There's a price. There always is, as well as a few more things you're going to have to ante up.

Chapter 10

NEXT-LEVEL NUANCES

*Managing the unseen and unspoken
subtleties of leading at the next level*

IN A FAMOUS Greek myth, Daedalus, a master craftsman, is fleeing Crete with his son, Icarus, due to some messy business involving a bull, a labyrinth, and the king's beautiful wife. To get them out of Dodge and fast, Daedalus fashions a most peculiar getaway vehicle: wings constructed from feathers and wax. When the two set out, Icarus keeps a low altitude, flying close to the water. Noting this, Daedalus warns his son against fear and insecurity. If Icarus flies too low, the sea will wet the wings, weigh them down, and he will drown. As Icarus gets more comfortable and confident, he flies higher and higher, and his father warns him again. This time, it's about hubris and arrogance and that flying too high will result in the sun's heat destroying the contraption of wax and feathers. Unfortunately, Icarus ignores his father and flies too close to the sun. Just as predicted, the wax melts, and Icarus falls and is swallowed up by the sea.

The myth discusses the tension between insecurity and arrogance. Between these tensions lives caution, confidence, readiness, impulsiveness, the dream, realistic expectations, risks, planning, urgency, and patience. It tells us that often success is found in the nuances, in the subtleties, and in the gray spaces in between. Proving your leadership mettle is no different. You know the leadership sequence: self-mastery, engaging and influencing, and causing change and adding value. You know that leadership targets different objects to impact: self, others, and business. You know that this impact manifests via a myriad of visible competencies. You know that leadership unfolds in a variety of contexts, each one requiring different combinations and degrees of competencies. And you know that walking in these competencies must be intentional. You must do these things on purpose if you are to create a positive association between you and what people recognize as leadership. Now it is time to apply what you know, but here's the caveat: you must do these things in a highly caffeinated world that moves faster than Japan's bullet train, The Shinkansen.

In some ways, ascending to the roles you want is a formulaic and straightforward equation. Some parts are a matter of simple arithmetic, like finding out what competencies your organization most values and embodying them. But in other ways, how those competencies will bend, twist, and take shape when applied in your fast moving reality involves a mysterious kind of calculus with hidden variables that don't always add up. Just like Icarus, you have to find just the right altitude to fly despite the tensions pulling you up towards the sun or down toward the sea. Compounding the challenge is that you must do this math with little time to contemplate it—and perhaps, in the face of incomplete data. With only your best judgment to rely on, you'll have to *feel* your way through—and fast.

Judgment Day

Years ago, when I worked in human resources (HR), one of my jobs was coaching coaches—that is, advising managers on how to solve employee problems. Although there was the usual fare of employee infractions, there was also a mysterious body of challenges that always fell under what the *theys* called judgment. *Judgment* is generally code for being appropriately responsive to the context in which your leadership is expected to unfold. That's reasonable, and when it is done well, it proves that a person is adept at navigating the subtleties of the work world—a clear sign of the individual's readiness to take the wheel and lead. What makes having good judgment so laudable is that it's much more than just doing what you're told and doing it well. Good judgment, even if you lack experience, takes plain-old good sense. It means the employee can navigate ambiguity with success. Although the employee may require experience or his or her manager's specific direction, the employee still manages to traverse a situation in which the rules of engagement are anything but clear. It's not just a matter of doing right. That's easy. Judgment is about doing right when you're not sure, given the context, what doing right means.

Back in HR, incidents involving poor judgment typically started with an employee who, despite being otherwise reliable, had behaved in some shocking, inexplicable, and highly inappropriate way—or so the managers in my office told it. It had often been in a high-stakes business situation, within the earshot of high-powered executives of influence, in a boardroom, or amid the morning bagels or afternoon lattes. Something embarrassing had tumbled from the mouth of the underexperienced underling. And the whole ugly thing had finally culminated in the distressed manager sitting in my office wanting help.

It would seem that addressing these kinds of problems would be simple. The HRian in me would immediately look to her handbook to ask, "What does the policy say? What were the manager's directions? What did the employee's training instruct?" Given all the guardrails within typical organizational policy, why, if the employee's infraction was so awful and easy to see, was the employee's boss sitting across the desk from me, shoulders shrugged, not knowing what to do? I'll tell you why: because rules of judgment aren't in the handbook. Navigating ambiguity isn't in the policy manual. These situations play out where the weather is cloudy and the road signs are few and far between.

Author Matthew Kelly wrote, "Everybody is a genius. But if you judge a fish by its ability to climb a tree, it will live its whole life believing that it is stupid."[22] Up-and-coming leaders are often judged by their ability to climb trees, although they likely have no experience with it. Good judgment, I came to understand, usually boiled down to the employee's ability to read rules that are unwritten, to see edicts that are invisible, to adhere to training the employee was never taught, and to fulfill expectations that are mostly unspoken.

Now let that sit and soak in for a moment. How can you be held accountable for directions, expectations, rules, training, and operating principles you were never given? That faint stink you smell is the reality that life is not fair. When rising leaders see their way through an ambiguous situation that is outside their experience, the *theys* call it good instinct. However, absent a mentor, coach, or nurturing manager, it is more likely the employee's good luck. Meanwhile, when rising leaders fail to decipher a situation and its social requirements correctly, even if the situation is outside their know-how, it is called poor judgment. There's no forgiveness or latitude for inexperience. The *theys* frown on it because, in their minds, the employee *should have known better*; the employee should have used common sense. Again, it's not fair—but those are the rules of the game.

New Rules, Different Game

The truth is, any employee can misread a situation and suffer some pain as a consequence. Employees on the rise, employees working to be seen as leaders and ready for the next level, however, have so much more at stake. You have more light on you. More people are watching. The expectations are muddier. As a leader on the rise, many think you are supposed to know better, be better, be brighter, and have keener instincts for such things. Especially from the vantage point of a manager's Monday morning quarterbacking, employees climbing to the next level should be able to read a situation and respond appropriately. Though you are a fish, if you're working towards what's next at work, the *theys* will expect you to climb trees.

The road to the next level is anything but simple, linear, or straight. In truth, it's a precarious journey of twists and turns. Most only learn how to navigate it through the bitter tutelage of experience. Although managers attempt to manufacture these slippery situations in training or simulations, they generally struggle. It's hard to choreograph all of the variables that contribute to the real world you have to walk and talk in. When you guess right, you get the badge of *good instincts* (whether true or not). But if you fail, you may be branded as having poor judgment. And what are you supposed to do with that label?

Experience is an effective teacher, but when it comes to growing your leadership chops, she's cruel and not at all fair. There is no playbook with which to unravel these riddles of circumstance. When all these elements converge, what to do can get murky. What's worse is that the average employee who is intent on climbing to the next level likely doesn't even know he or she has stepped into it—this new world, with a new game, and its different rules of engagement. The office looks the way it always did. The people are the same people. The tasks are the same tasks. What is different is you.

If you're climbing to a next-level role, know that you are operating under a unique set of rules. If you're climbing, know that you're auditioning—all of the time. You are on stage—all of the time. The stakes are higher, and the rewards are more profitable. The ambiguities are grayer. The cost is more expensive, and the lights on you are brighter than ever. You're stuck in a vexing catch-22, in which the moniker of poor judgment will be the convenient catchall and cold consequence for any missteps you will inevitably make on your ascent up the career ladder. You're just going to be held to a higher standard. The good news is that you can lower the risks and the temperature, if you have the benefit of what you're about to learn.

Exposé

If visibility, competency's lil' helper, is the light you need for your leadership abilities to shine as evident and recognizable, then it's important we discuss your ability to tolerate the heat once you're on stage and under the lamp. Consider the objects your leadership impacts, self, others, and business, each requiring ascending levels of leadership competency. Each of these different contexts, as if they were theater stages on which you act out your leadership, will make different demands on you. The first and smallest stage is like theater in the park. You're acting, but it's low pressure; under a pleasant afternoon sun; and happening before a small, friendly, and accommodating audience. The third and the biggest stage is like playing New York City's Lincoln Center, behind a big marquee, below bright lights, and with the eyes of savvy sophisticates and critics all on you. Every performance is high pressure, as stardom looms—and if not, oblivion. And there's the middle, bigger than the first, smaller than the third, holding some comforts and some risks of the two at the extremes.

The first signs of having good judgment are often seen when a leader simply performs at a level that his or her competencies and heat tolerance can support. Good judgment is easy when an actor knows what size stage he or she can handle. That sounds simple, but think about the degree of intention, self-awareness, and humility that requires. First, you have to know, really *know*, who you are and what you can do. Then you need to have the self-control and discernment to keep yourself in circumstances that challenge your leadership muscle to the appropriate degree. Venture into a context that overchallenges your readiness and you will look like a novice. Show up in a context that underchallenges your readiness and you will seem cowardly, like someone who refuses to rise to his or her potential, or just plain lazy.

As Goldilocks instructed, for leadership to be evident, it must show up in situations that are not too big for it, nor too small. You have to demonstrate leadership in situations that are just right. Bite off more than your leadership competencies can chew (or too little), and the price can be the scarlet brand of poor judgment. But that's not how it happens. You getting to choose what to bite into or not, isn't how it happens. More often, circumstances surprise you with an unexpected test of your judgment. More often, you don't even realize you are in the thick of it. You are minding your own business, unsuspecting, and completely caught off guard. But whether you walked into a test of judgment—or fell in, success will rely on you striking the right posture and pose—and just so you know, it's a profile shot.

High Profile

At times, employees who are endeavoring to prove their leadership readiness fail because they cannot withstand the heat of leading at certain ranks. They don't have the profile for it. Your leadership profile reflects the experiential and social supports that give you the tolerance to withstand the heat, exposure, and expectations of leadership at different levels. Profile, however, is a double-edged sword. On the one hand, a leadership profile is like sunscreen: the more you have, the stronger you are, and the better you can manage the heat of the environments in which you are leading. But on the other hand, your leadership profile, an element of your brand, advertises your strengths or limitations, for better or for worse.

Your leadership profile, told through your brand, defines what *should* be the breadth of your capability—and also the limits. It tells the *theys* what they *should* anticipate seeing from you, what you *might* be capable of, what *may* be within your reach to deliver, and what may not. Whether "what they *should* anticipate," "what you *might* be capable of," and "what you *may* deliver" falls within or outside your reality is immaterial. Rightly or wrongly, your profile, sets other people's expectations of you.

In the years before I struck out on my own as a coach and independent consultant, I had the good sense to get myself prepared. Well, in truth, it wasn't *my* good sense exactly; I borrowed it. I was fortunate to have several good mentors and coaches who loaned their good sense to me. Like an investment, my eventual success would pay it back and, I'd like to think, pay it forward as I help others. One piece of great advice was to pursue and earn diverse professional credentials. That meant engaging in long, arduous training programs and assessments that tested my growing competencies. It was painful and tedious, and at times, I questioned why I was putting myself through it. But I prayed the payoff was worth its cost in years, in learning, in failing, in trying, in bruised knees, and in a bruised behind—all in hopes that I would eventually emerge with a concrete set of bona fides that would communicate that I wasn't just calling myself a coach and a consultant. My profile would say to the world that I could do precisely what I claimed I could do.

You will recall that a single competency is loaded with several skills and abilities that work together to create that competency as a result. Your leadership profile has a similar function. Your profile is shorthand for all of the skills, sets of experience, and capabilities you have. It tells the story of what you can handle, what you *have* handled, and whether you can be trusted to handle more. Think of a higher leadership profile as having the ability to fly closer to the sun while being considerably better prepared than Icarus.

When you have a higher profile, you have more visibility, more reach, and a broader opportunity to shine and prove yourself. However, having a higher leadership profile isn't all sunshine. More light means more scrutiny. It means many people are watching, each with expectations, which creates more risk and a wider opportunity for the *theys* to see you stumble and fall. Conversely, a lower leadership profile suggests you have more visible competencies to master. It means there is less light on you, and that means less risk, pain, and rejection. But it also means less visibility and fewer opportunities to be seen by the decision-making *theys*. You have limited reach with a lower profile, and you likely have fewer chances to prove you are a rising star. Your profile isn't cement, however; it can shift, move, and change. If your profile is lower than you'd like, don't fret. You can still get your shot. You may just need to make your own luck. And in the meantime, avoid overplaying your hand.

Alignment, Yet Again

Your eyes are bigger than your stomach. It's a tried-and-true saying uttered by moms, dads, and grandparents when children load up a plate with fried, juicy, drippy, cheesy, crunchy, and whipped-cream good stuff and then struggle to consume all that their eyes desired. My question to you is this: Is your ambition bigger than your profile? Do you want more position than you have profile to manage it?

The elements that comprise a person's profile—his or her visible competencies, the object his or her leadership most often impacts, and the context in which that leadership most often operates—must all align (see figure 6). For example, if the *theys* are looking for someone to fill a manager role, requiring a moderate-level profile, the recruiter will be on the lookout for people who can successfully operate in a leading others context—and that so happens to require at least a moderate degree of visible competencies. If the *theys* want to identify the next senior vice president for grooming and development, it means a higher degree of visible competencies will be expected. It follows, then, that the recruiters will be on the hunt for people whose profiles reflect a burgeoning midlevel executive who can easily lead others and business.

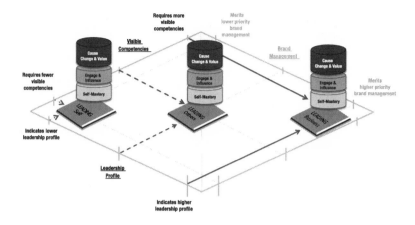

Fig. 6. Higher Leadership Profile Aligns with Larger Objects of Impact and Higher Degrees of Visible Competency

Visible competencies. Leadership profile. Brand management. All leadership indicators generally run in the same direction. Leaders who are primarily leading self (e.g., doers), which requires fewer visible competencies, have a lower profile and hence, do not have to prioritize brand management (see figure 7). Meanwhile, leaders who are leading others (e.g., managing enablers and SMEs or nonmanaging enablers) will need to demonstrate more visible competencies to support their moderate profile. Moderate attention to brand management helps also (see figure 8). The same alignment occurs for senior managers (e.g., strategists). They are expected to demonstrate mastery of more visible leadership competencies that will serve as the backbone of their high leadership profile. And it's that high profile that, for them, merits brand management being a top priority (see figure 9).

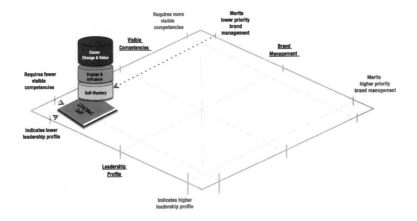

Fig. 7. Lower Levels of Leadership Competency, Profile, and Brand Management Aligned around Leading Self

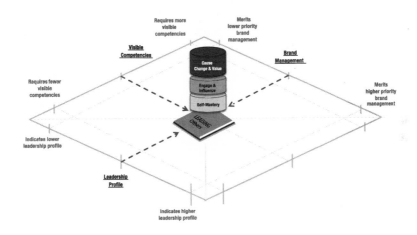

Fig. 8. Moderate Levels of Leadership Competency, Profile, and Brand Management Aligned around Leading Others

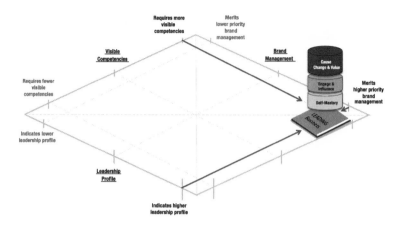

Fig. 9. Higher Levels of Leadership Competency, Profile, and
Brand Management Aligned around Leading Business

When there are misalignments, like when a person of one profile leads in a role or in a context that is either too big or too small, you can be sure there's a hidden element in play. A person of a smaller profile in a bigger-context role is probably being developed *up*. They are being groomed and grown. Maybe they are part of a facilitated development program or aligned with a coach. But notice what should always come with the coupling of smaller profile-bigger context: support. When operating in a context higher than one's profile, it is advisable to have a high-level sponsor (e.g., a manager or high ranking mentor) to support in the background by providing cover and coaching. Otherwise, though not intentionally, that ambition is being set up to fall, hit, and crack on the ground.

Conversely, when you see a person with a big profile leading in a smaller context—something's, something's just not right. And that could mean a few things: he or she has been demoted *down*. Perhaps he or she has outgrown the role. The work has been misallocated, or the leader has been ill-placed in the wrong position. Leadership favors alignment. Ideally, the role at the center of your ambition should be compatible with the profile it will take to be successful in it. But what if you're in a hurry? What if your ambition just can't wait?

Slow your roll. As a baby, you crawled before you walked, and you walked before you ran. As you chase what's next at work, it's tempting to want to leapfrog from where you are to where you want to be. It's tempting to want to hop over the position that sits in front of the role you really want. Whether growth occurs rapidly or one small step at a time, the most sustainable growth happens incrementally. Along the ordered steps toward what you want are crucial opportunities to get experience and development and, through these, raise your profile—which both protects you as well as proclaims your readiness. Significant gaps between a person's profile and the leadership context in which he or she wishes to lead can pose considerable risks for a leader on the rise. Even if your ambition tells you it is the right place for you to be, the question is whether you have the right stuff to be there.

The Right Stuff

Of what is your leadership profile made?

Visibility is the degree to which the impacts of your leadership will be seen or felt by others. Win or lose, how big is the audience of onlookers? Who will witness your ultimate success or failure: just you, your customers, or your boss (lower profile)? Or the department, the enterprise, or the whole community (higher profile)?

Object of impact describes the circumstantial stage on which your leadership will play out. Are you leading self and thus the only one impacted by your show of leadership (lower profile)? Or are you leading business, affecting the entire organization (higher profile)?

Gravitas describes your command and influence, especially among the most senior-level people in the organization. Gravitas is accomplished by demonstrating enough presence that any differences in official hierarchy dissolve under your ability to be seen as credible and of high value. Your influence extending only to a group of individual contributors or peers (lower profile) is very different from you being able to hold court and move the will of the CEO or the entire executive leadership team (higher profile).

Accountability is the condition of being responsible for the success or failure of a result, regardless of your actual involvement. In the elements mentioned previously, a leader having and retaining *more* personal visibility, *more* personal gravitas, and individually managing a *more* significant object are all indicators of a higher-profile leader. But accountability or ownership changes this pattern. For a high-profile leader, less is more:

Shared wins describes the extent to which you distribute the wins and rewards. Who will experience the fruits of winning? Higher-profile leaders share their victories with their teams and partners, assuming *less* of the credit. Lower-profile leaders claim more of the victory for themselves.

Owned loss describes the extent to which you are able and willing to solely absorb the blame and loss of a failure. In failure, who will feel the pain and the blame? Higher-profile leaders own and absorb risks and losses (at least publicly), putting *less* of the onus on the team. Lower-profile leaders share risks with their team members and their managers.

Breadth of representation is the extent to which you are in a position to speak for or act as an agent for a larger group or enterprise. Higher-profile leaders often speak on behalf of a group. When envisioning the future or when celebrating a win, these leaders often use pronouns like *our, we, us*—words that signify their membership in a larger group, *reducing* their identity as an individual. But in a situation where there has been a loss or a failure, higher-profile leaders will use pronouns that *shrink* the scope of the blame—*mine, my*, or *I*—to signify their individual ownership of the trouble.

If we analyze the case of Petra, the market development director, for clues about her profile, some interesting things emerge. In building up the organization's presence in the community, Petra is leading at the broadest level: business. In victory or defeat, whatever Petra does, many people will witness it, many people will be impacted, a lot of money is at stake, and her career is poised for great risk if the venture fails or great reward if it succeeds. Given Petra's position, in defeat, the stakeholders wouldn't blame one of the associates on her team. Even if one of her staff members proved to be the origin of the problem, it wouldn't matter. The blame would be Petra's, and she alone would have to answer for it. Conversely, in a win, she couldn't take all the credit. As a higher-profile leader, she would be expected to share the win between herself, her partners, and her hardworking team.

If we look at Trey, the information technology subject-matter expert, however, we see that although his profile is ascending, he doesn't have the lowest profile or the highest. This mix of higher- and lower-order elements in his profile could both shield Trey and expose him depending on who is pressing for accountability.

You will remember that Trey is leading others on an informal cross-functional team in IT as they rebuild the systems that will help groups in the department work more efficiently. Although less than Petra, Trey is under a lot of scrutiny too. If IT runs better, so does the organization. Thus, in some ways, the eyes of the whole enterprise are also watching. But here is where the lower-order elements of Trey's profile show themselves and shield him. If Trey fails to lead the project to success, the enterprise executives will look at the IT leadership for the answer—not Trey. The enterprise executives don't know Trey. The enterprise executives only have a commitment from their own direct reports: the senior leaders in IT (who, in turn, delegated the task to Trey). As far as the enterprise executives are concerned, it's: *Trey who?*

Meanwhile, Trey directly answers to IT leadership, and they expect him, as this informal work team's leader, to use departmental resources prudently to cause a successful result. These local line of business executives wouldn't abide Trey, with and through the work team, wasting their time, money, or efforts. If Trey fails to leverage his department's resources toward a success, it will not be the individuals on Trey's team who will have to answer for it—it will be Trey alone. It is true that broadly, in the enterprise, Trey has a lower profile. But locally, in his line of business, Trey's profile is higher, and he alone, not his work team, would have to stand in front of some high-powered IT folks with a lot of explaining to do.

We know that Kat, the analyst in finance, worked hard to get her snarkiness in check. This effort, in turn, strengthened her relationships and standing in the team. The team infighting stopped. The communication bottlenecks dissolved. The downstream benefits appeared. The production of analytics to various departments around the enterprise flowed like water. What if an internal department, so impressed by the uptick in the quality of their analytics, emailed a message of high praise? Who would get the email? And on whom would the email be focused? Likely, not Kat—in either case. The first to get the note would be Kat's boss, and the message would likely laud the work of the team in general. But we know Kat's boss to be a good manager, as evidenced by his willingness to develop her, so we could probably count on him to pass part of the praise to Kat as a way of reinforcing this employee's positive response to feedback. However, given Kat's lower profile, her individual improvement is likely not discernable to anyone beyond the borders of her immediate team.

Upside-Down World

We speculate that Petra is prepared to own the outcomes of her team, as is Trey, while Kat is content with the praise from her manager. But what if these three make different decisions? What if they, with each of their next-level goals still in place, ignore the rules of context and profile? What if Petra passes blame to her lower-ranking subordinates for a failure she is supposed to own? What if Trey decides he does not have to be a good steward of the IT department's resources and squanders them all, then calls it the fault of his work team? What if Kat pouts and tantrums because the internal customer's note of praise doesn't laud her personally? Each one will have severely damaged their evident readiness to lead or lead at a higher level. And why? In our upside-down world, each one has failed to appropriately estimate what each one's profile can cover.

Petra is a senior leader in a high-stakes, enterprise-impacting game, yet in our upside-down world, she behaves like a doer. Trey is a senior professional. He wants to steer the work of many, but he sidesteps responsibility like he's one of the gang. Kat is an individual contributor—she is only leading herself—but she wants praise as if she were leading a large team. In this upside-down world, in each case, the math doesn't add up: the rules of their hierarchical or situational context, the size of their profiles, and what they do or expect don't add up. These are the kind of judgment failures that kill the rise of leaders. These errors of judgment complicate and undo your brand—your efforts to be seen and valued as a leader who's ready for what's next at work. Poor judgment is often the result of people ignoring the rules of context, over- or underestimating their leadership profile, displaying behaviors, or having expectations that don't align. Readiness to lead means holding symmetry between these three elements: the hierarchical or situational context you are in, the appropriate behaviors and expectations thereof, and an accurate estimate of what your leadership profile can bear. When all of those align, your brand can tell and foretell your success story. And the *theys* are listening.

Scaling Up

Fake it 'til you make it. You have likely heard this saying before. It is not one of my favorites because although its words may be clear, what to do about it isn't. I understand that it is encouraging you not to let the fact that you don't know everything you need to know—keep you from an opportunity. Not knowing all the steps shouldn't prevent you from attending the dance. However, many people think it means to act *as if* or to pretend you are ready for the role when you're not, hoping no one notices. Let me tell you something: they'll notice!

Through the lens of the conversation you and I are having, this saying is urging you to operate outside of what your profile can support. If you want to dress the part, fine. If you want to learn and study the part, great! But if you're going to *lead* in a part that is bigger than your profile can support, consider this first. Leadership, as we have discussed, walks and talks, but it does something else first: it thinks! It is aware. It assesses the situation. Leaders think well before they *act as if* or act any other kind of way. You want to scale up and climb to the next level. I get it; but first, recognize where you are. First, understand the *distance* between where you are and where you want to be. First, understand the *difference* between where you are and where you want to be. In that distance, in that difference, is nuance, context, good judgment, and leadership profile. Let's examine the situation of Jacob, the client specialist, a little closer because, like some of you, he wants to scale up too.

Jacob led by helping a senior and customer navigate the new design of her statement. His leadership had a positive impact. We can see that Jacob followed the leadership sequence perfectly in that he self-managed, engaged, and influenced, which helped him cause a change and add value. But if we examine his leadership for the elements of leadership profile, we see a bit more:

- *Who was impacted or affected?* The immediate customer.

- *How many people did he have to influence?* Just one.

- *What risk did the change pose?* Although the outcome was positive, the risk was probably minimal.

- *Degree of accountability?* At a minimum, Jacob is accountable for the experience of his customers. At maximum, perhaps it would have been escalated up to his boss.

- *What reward did his leadership offer?* One satisfied customer and a saved account.

- *What about visibility and people having a line of sight*

into Jacob's win or loss? It's low. Although the outcome was positive, outside Jacob and his customer, no one will see it.

Given these facts alone, how much heat or exposure does Jacob have to tolerate? That's obvious: not much. Thus, how reasonable would it be for Jacob to expect the *theys* to see him as ready for a next-level position, like managing a group of his own? That's obvious too: not very. His leadership profile doesn't match the size or the expected impact of someone who is a people manager or operating in the leading-others context. Yes, Jacob led himself and did it well, but that's his job. It's not realistic to be seen as promotable for merely doing your job. Again, this goes to minding your expectations around your promotability based on the profile you have now.

Strategic Reflection No. 24

In the space provided, write down the leadership position to which you aspire. Be detailed. Itemize which people the role impacts and how it adds value. Describe the scope of the influence it will have. Discuss its visibility and the gravitas required for it. Will it require you to lead self, others, the business, or a combination? What does the role have to be accountable for? And to whom?

_____

_____

_____

_____

_____

_____

_____

Now think about your current leadership profile. How much visibility and gravitas do you currently have? What is the most frequent object of your leadership's impact? How willing are you to share successes with a large number of people? How ready are you to absorb the risk or failures, although those failures may not be your own?

_____

_____

_____

_____

_____

_____

_____

Lay the role you want beside the leadership profile you currently have. If your leadership profile remains exactly as it is, how realistic is your expectation to be a viable candidate for that next-level role?

_____

_____

_____

_____

_____

_____

Let's up the ante on Jacob, the client specialist. He wants to scale up and lead at a higher level. He knows that won't happen for just doing what he is supposed to do. But what happens when Jacob *fakes it until he makes it* or *acts as if?* Imagine that one morning, Jacob, feeling extra-bold after an extra-strong espresso, creates a cheat sheet that deciphers the new statements. After all, *continuously seeking and pursuing ways to innovate* is what leaders do. Then, once his second espresso kicks in, Jacob, deciding he needs to *act as if* and *help people transition to the new normal*—another thing leaders do—sends it to every single customer doing business with the company.

There you have it: Jacob scaling up. *Nailed it!* Right? Well, I'll just say it like this: I wouldn't want to be Jacob when his boss finds out; or when his boss' boss finds out; or when the marketing department, the compliance department, and the legal department find out. What happened to *act as if* and *fake it 'til you make it?* Jacob's attempt to demonstrate his leadership was too big. His low leadership profile can't support it. Jacob attempted to act like a higher-level leader, but he failed *to think* like one. Thinking like a higher-level leader would have included mindfulness around regulatory-, reputational-, and legal impacts as well as other ramifications. Jacob, although *acting as if,* is not at all prepared to manage all the actions he took. His intention of wanting to help his customer is laudable, but his boss will undoubtedly call this move poor judgment due to the fact that Jacob does not have the profile to pull it off. Yes, the *theys* will notice him, but for all the wrong reasons.

> ## An Insider Tip
> ## When Scaling up, You Need
> ## a Ticket to Ride
>
> *For some roles, trying to scale up and exhibit leadership in a next-level context can be risky. Leading outside the bounds of your role could be seen as going rogue, being arrogant, or challenging the chain of command.*
>
> *If you want a next-level position, first make it known to your boss. Remember, to cause change that adds value, you must first self-manage to influence the aid of others, in this case, your manager. Tell your manager you are interested in being developed for upward growth. Get clear on what you want, why—and use that clarity to make a precise ask.*
>
> *Work with your manager to engage in stretch assignments or development efforts that give you next-level experiences, while not fully exposing you—or your manager—to next-level risks. These assignments are usually of ever-increasing difficulty, as well as impact, influence, and accountability—the same elements that not only grow your skills but also grow your profile.*

That's the beauty of stretch assignments: you get experience and exposure, without the high price of being up the creek with no paddle.

Psst! I shouldn't tell you this, but stretch assignments, in addition to being a growth opportunity for the up-and-coming leader, also serve the theys as a scouting opportunity. These assignments often put you in front of people in the organization who are quietly looking for rising talent. If you see an opportunity to lead up, first align with your manager so that he or she can provide support, sponsorship, coaching, political protection, and air cover. Remember, to be seen as a leader, you need visibility. When you engage your manager to sponsor your upward movement, you situate someone to witness the leader you could be while he or she protects the leader you are.

Let's try this one more time. It's the same situation, but what does Jacob actually do?

Case Study: Jacob, Senior Client Specialist, Customer Service

After he successfully closed the call with his initially upset customer, Jacob wonders how unique her frustration was. Maybe it was just her—Ja-

cob's elderly client, or maybe the confusion is more universal. As Jacob decides to pay attention and note the pattern of his own customers' complaints, he brings the potential problem to his manager and asks if he may invite all the client specialist to do the same. The manager's curiosity is piqued, and Jacob gets the okay. Later, with the data he and his peers collected in hand, Jacob presents the findings to his boss and proposes a solution. Jacob leads his presentation with his concern for the "customer experience"—one of his manager's favorite phrases. If Jacob had his manager's curiosity before, now Jacob has his undivided attention.

While it is a well deserved win, Jacob getting promoted on the strength of this one effort is unlikely. But noticing the problem and collecting the empirical data to bear it out, let alone building a proposal on a solution framed around his manager's favorite success measure, is a great start. Suddenly, Jacob's not just leading self like an ordinary customer service rep. Suddenly, he is thinking like a higher-level leader and driving value in a higher-level context. Note that Jacob does not execute on the data he collects. That's because he can't. It's not appropriate given his position. He simply doesn't have the profile to support taking the idea the full distance. However, he doesn't have to. It doesn't matter that he isn't at the higher level; he just needs to think like a leader at that level would. Remember the leadership sequence. By staying in his profile lane, Jacob self manages. He can still cause positive change and value with and through others—like his manager, who *does* have the profile to carry the idea further. And for that, the *theys* are likely to begin seeing Jacob in an entirely different light.

> ## An Insider Tip
> ## Raising Your Leadership Profile
>
> *Growing your leadership profile is a matter of engaging in a leadership development strategy, a plan by which you can incrementally grow your leadership muscle and exposure safely over time because growth, not mastery, is the focus. If you want to be a leader others can increasingly see, appreciate, and reward, development is a must. With development comes the ability to tolerate more heat and the ability to convert heat into fuel to launch you further.*
>
> *A leadership development strategy should include three primary components. 10% of your development strategy should go toward educating yourself about leadership or the domain in which you will lead. Training classes, development programs, and books are the usual courses of action. 20% of your development strategy should engage learning with and through others, such as direct support from a manager, mentor, or coach. 70% of your development strategy, however, should come through experience—you walking*

and talking in situations that allow you to practice leadership in real time. Learning by doing, which generally includes a great deal of social contact as well, is the most effective way of learning and exercising the craft of leadership.

Again, leverage your relationships, especially the one with your manager, who is the likeliest person to give you access to experiment in situations that will exercise your leadership abilities. For example, if you want to grow into a people management role, you might, as part of your leadership development strategy, begin coaching the new employees or the junior members of the team. Like all leadership, your ability to cause change and add value hinges on your ability to influence the relationships around you.

Look for opportunities that will specifically test and expand your current capabilities. Unfortunately, discomfort is part of the deal. Look at these growing pains as signals that you are treading closely to and beyond your former learning edge. To get more means you have to go further than you have ever been.

Getting Started

The goal of this chapter is not to encourage you to lower your career goals but, rather, to up your game. Embracing the tactics involved in managing context and the contextual boundaries of your profile are critical to you being seen as a serious contender for a next-level position. If the role you want and the role you are prepared for (as evidenced by your current profile) are mismatched, you have some decisions to make. You can identify a different aspiration that matches the profile you have, or you can grow into the position you want through a strategic leadership development plan. With development comes the ability to tolerate and use the heat of a higher profile to propel you further along your career journey.

I once heard a graphic designer say, "It's not good unless it looks good." He was talking about the marriage between something *actually* being a bona fide quality product and it *looking like* one. If something doesn't look good, even if it is good, most people won't go through the effort of proving their first impression wrong. If you don't look ready for a next-level opportunity, even if you believe you are, most people won't go through the effort of proving their first impression about you wrong.

In the culinary business, it's said that we *first eat with our eyes*. In the business of identifying talent for opportunities at work, career decision-makers *first choose with their eyes*. It's as much about you *looking* ready as it is about you *being* ready. Building your leadership profile that shines through your brand, along with your capability that can back it up, helps you to *look* ready and to *be* worthy for what's next at work. Then, the only thing left to do is wait.

Chapter 11

IN THE MEANTIME

Considerations en route to the next level

NAVIGATING YOUR JOURNEY toward getting ahead at work is a game of chess, not checkers. Like chess, your passage upward should be deliberate and mindful while you engage in what will be an intricate dance of concentration, patience, and strategy. Your desire for a next-level job is just one minor piece on an elaborate board of factors that must align like stars in the constellations. Although this book shows that you can influence many of those celestial bodies, other determinants are beyond your sphere of influence. Enterprise performance, stock price, revenue health, the competitor landscape, business-cycle stage, and the departmental budget are just some of the factors that can influence the availability of next-level opportunities in your organization. Finding a balance between moving the things you can, along with understanding the nature of the things you cannot, is a must on the journey toward revealing the leader you really are. This strategic patience is your ability to accept and tolerate delay, but don't ever confuse it with passivity. Strategic patience does not mean sitting still—waiting for lightning to strike. For a leader like you, there's plenty to keep you busy so that you're in position and ready when it does.

Power and Politics

Leadership guru Peter F. Drucker wrote, "The organization is, above all, social. It is people."[23] Take away the bricks and mortar of the building in which you work, take away the elaborate technological systems, and even take away the products and the customers. What remains are the people— your organization's employees, your coworkers—each of whom wants and needs to get things done at multiple points on any given day.

You've read it here before: nothing is possible in isolation. To achieve anything at work, you need the assistance, approval, cooperation, attention, awareness, consumption, energy, engagement, and effort of others. Think about them: all of the people in and around where you work, each one trying to move someone else, all trying to influence what they want into being. In this way, all of these people are identical. However, a critical differentiator among them is the social power to get what they want. Only a few have it. Only a few of these people have the currency of social power to draw to themselves what they want and need at work. Meanwhile, there are many more who do not have it. What's the next best thing to having the social leverage to unlock what you want and need? Having relationships with the people who do. This balance of having power or having it via your relationships is the essence of politics: social power at work—building it, getting it, and keeping it, and if you can't do any of those, aligning with the people who can.

Politics isn't a bad word. It's just a way of talking about leveraging our social connections into the relationship currency that helps us negotiate our way through a career. Relationship currency is the outcome of having the social access and ability to give and take mutual resources from a social connection. Workplace politics is simply the process by which that exchange unfolds. And all of us, in our ways, engage in it. We have connections at work that benefit us. At their maximum, these relationships can result in our having direct access to tangible opportunities like jobs and seats on plum assignments. At a minimum, these relationships entertain us, keep us company, or sit with us at lunch. We informally learn and teach through politics. Even gossiping, as wicked as it may seem, is a way of teaching us, often through someone else's error, what the unwritten social rules of conduct are and are not. Any way you cut it, in big and small ways, relationships are conduits to power—the power of access, the power of community, and the power of information.

Although we all leverage our relationships for one reason or another, politicking gets a bad rap. The manager who brings coffee and doughnuts for the team on Fridays is politicking. The employee who offers the boss a new idea or a new twist on an old one is politicking. The person who listens to the same mind-numbing story about a cubicle mate's stamp collection, all for the sake of keeping the relationship in good stead, is politicking. In and of itself, politicking is no sin. Manipulation, gamesmanship, and duplicity are, and are unfortunate political devices to accelerate or deepen one's social access to power. But take heed; their use will cut into your integrity and hurt the state of your leadership brand. Conversely, practicing the art of making and maintaining social alignments that give you degrees of social control over your circumstances, along with direct or indirect access to the things you want and need at work, is just smart. So long as it results in mutualistic wins at no one's expense, politicking is a normal function of relationships where power is involved. Mutualistic politics is where everyone in the relationship walks away unharmed, at the least, and at most with the thing they bargained for, all while keeping all hands on the table and open.

Managing Up

I hate to be the one to tell you, but you are political too. If you have a manager and you work in any small or large ways to keep yourself in his or her good graces, you're political. And there is not a thing wrong with that. In fact, you'd be silly to behave in any other way. Of all the *theys* whose advocacy you need to climb, your boss is among the most important. In that relationship, you want to be seen as a benefit, and there are times when it's a relationship from which you will want to be able to draw benefits. Like any other, this connection thrives on the gifts of mutual wins, where both you and your manager benefit. What you want out of the relationship is clear; this book is built around it. But what does your boss want?

That's clear too. Your manager wants what everyone wants. Managers want to look smart and capable, like they and the group they manage are adding value to the organization. And there are things they don't want. They don't want to be embarrassed; they don't want to be humiliated. They don't want their strategic direction or the goals for which they are responsible to be undermined. There's nothing too exotic about that, is there? Of course not. And the cooperative path to bring a manager's wants into fruition is usually easy for an ordinary employee to follow. He or she simply needs to say yes, and execute. But you are not an ordinary employee. You are a leader on the rise, aware that your leadership unfolds at various levels, impacting different people, groups, or the organization as a whole. You also know that each of those contexts is unique, as is what being a value-add will mean and look like. Suddenly what used to be simple, like satisfying your manager's expectations, has grown complex.

The key to becoming a critical asset to your boss, the person who can have the most direct impact on your positive movement, isn't about puckering or pandering up; it's about *partnering up*. One of the best perks high-value employees report enjoying is when they sense their managers have given them peer status—that is, when managers treat them not like an employee but like a peer or a trusted advisor. Employees who reach this level of relationship get unique attention, time, coaching, and access, and most importantly, they get heard. These employees' points of view have weight. These employees have direct influence on the work. These employees get autonomy because they are trusted. These employees get opportunities because they are capable. These employees are prized because they are indispensible.

An Insider Tip
How to be Indispensable

Become your Manager's Consultant. *Based on the premise of change your mind, and the rest will follow, try this Jedi mind trick—not on your boss, on yourself. Just for a moment, stop thinking of yourself as your manager's employee, and start thinking of your boss as your client. Just for a moment, stop thinking of yourself as an employee, and start thinking of yourself as a consultant. What would you do for a client that you may be less inclined to do for a manager? What would you do as your manager's consultant that you might be less willing to do as an everyday employee?*

A consultant would ask more questions to get a sense of what the client's priorities and concerns are. A consultant would be keen to demonstrate valuable expertise when it is strategically beneficial. A consultant would make well-thought-out recommendations. A consultant would anticipate beyond the current assignments and also deliver on the next logical step. A consultant doesn't need to personally like the client to serve him or her, or the project impeccably. And a consultant would evaluate his or her own results to provide evidence of the value-add he or she delivered. This shift in your thinking isn't something you announce. It is simply a different way of activating your walk, talk, and self-image as a leader.

Parrot your Manager's Concerns. *We give ourselves away all the time. If you pay attention to what someone says, does, and spends his or her energy on, you can discern what that person cares most about. What does your manager talk about most often? What does your manager worry about most of the time? On what are the manager's questions mostly focused? What, in your manager's mind, defines success? Staying on budget? Customer satisfaction? Being in sync with best and next industry practices? Use that focus to inform all your deliverables. For example, if your manager is a budget hawk, for him or her, it's all about the money. With that in mind, your next presentation deck should include data that is all about the money. Although you would situate all other pertinent information in the body of your presentation deck, front-load or lead with the budgetary implications. Make sure the budget data sits close to the beginning of the report or is highlighted in an executive summary. Suddenly, your manager is listening to a presentation that is specially designed to speak directly to his or her most pressing concerns. Suddenly, you're not just another employee; suddenly, you're someone your manager would say, "gets me."*

Zoned Out

Case Study: Jacob, Client Specialist, Customer Service

It's now been a few weeks since Jacob's research and proposal activated a change to the customer statements his organization distributed. In the glow of that win, Jacob approaches his boss about being groomed for more responsibility. Jacob wants to take on a supervisory role, and he wants his boss' help to get ready. His manager agrees, and together they design a development plan that will invite Jacob to operate outside his comfort zone. Jacob will have to talk to people he's not used to talking to. He'll have to make decisions he's not used to making. He'll have to try things he's never experienced. Jacob will have to wade into murky ambiguity and the unknown.

What if Jacob says no? What if Jacob, who says he wants to climb to the next level, is unwilling to face this gauntlet where his current abilities—and likely his ego—will be tested? What if the prospect of that temporary discomfort and awkwardness is just too high a price for him? What will happen? The answer is, nothing will happen. Absolutely. Nothing. Will. Happen.

Everything costs; climbing to next-level positions costs. Climbing upward to lead in a bigger context or to build your leadership profile means turning up the heat to which you are exposed. It will mean exchanging being an experienced expert relative to the job you have now for becoming an awkward student of the role you want—at least at first. It is a well-understood fact among HRians that promoting even a high-achieving employee to an advanced role will result in a temporary dip in that employee's performance. It's to be expected as that employee learns the scope and responsibilities of the new position. Whereas being an expert got the employee promoted, only his or her willingness to become a learner will keep that employee there. Heat and discomfort come with next-level roles, so get comfortable with being uncomfortable. Get comfortable with sitting in the gray of ambiguity. If you can't take the heat, and if you're unwilling to lean into the lessons and self-awareness that discomfort has to teach you, stay out of the kitchen and far away from higher-profile roles.

Luigi's

We have been following the case of Petra, the director of market development. Let's hone in on a particular detail. When it came to expanding the company's presence, Petra went after one community, and she won. However, if she takes that one win, as wonderful as it was, and tries to parlay it into a next-level promotion, she'll likely lose. Why? One victory isn't enough to prove that you're ready to step up. And there's another reason. A popular motivational quote is: "Every new level of your life will require a new you." The next-level role Petra wants will require more from her: more influencing, more impacting, and more risk-taking—and tolerance to harsher light. The next level role she wants will require a new Petra. This evolution doesn't need to take place overnight, however. Like loan officers, the *theys* will extend *credit* and time to rising leaders and take chances on their talent, but only for those who demonstrate they are a smart bet and are already halfway where a promotion would take them.

In my hometown, there's a famous little pizza spot tucked away on the north side. The pizza is so good, your stomach will come up and kiss your mouth for the favor. It is the place to get a piping-hot slice, especially on a Friday night of fun with friends. But even on a school night, you can get an almost-baked pie to throw in the oven at home and—voilà—fifteen minutes later, enjoy just as if they had served it up fresh in the restaurant. The *theys* at work—HRians and hiring managers—are busy people. Rather than growing a leader from scratch or buying talent from the outside who will need to acclimate to a new employer, they have a keen eye for internal leadership talent that is already almost cooked and almost fully functional. But how does one do that? How do you prove you're a leader who just needs a few more minutes in the oven before you're ready?

For Petra, demonstrating her role mastery meant expanding the organization's footprint into one underserved market. Check! But Petra knows one win just constitutes her doing her job. She will need to do more, within an appropriate scope, to show she is next-level ready. First, she would need to determine what the next level is or could be. Now we're talking retail development, the job of market expansion; or community outreach, the job of building alliances in the local government and municipality; or mergers and acquisitions, the task of sniffing out peer or competitor organizations that are ripe for purchase—or a role that involves all three. Once Petra determines—even loosely—what a next-level position could be, it is a good time for her to learn about the next-level expectations attached to it. Upon discovering this new or upgraded mix of competencies, Petra needs to integrate them, where appropriate, into her current walk and talk in ways that add business value. As mentioned earlier, Petra would do well to involve her manager or a mentor in her plans—not just for the coaching and guidance, but also because she needs a witness. Petra needs someone of clout and internal influence to witness as she transforms into an almost-cooked and a nearly functional candidate for what's bigger and better at work.

Keep Delivering

On the road toward next-level leadership, you, like Petra, must exist in parallel universes. You have a foot in the world of the leader you want to be: thinking like it, walking like it, and talking like it so that the *theys* see you as promising, almost cooked, and all but ready for the next level. However, as you nurture what *will be*, remember that you also have a foot and a vested interest in *what is*.

Along this journey, I have invited you to engage and leverage your manager as a partner. When is the optimal time to do this? In the glow of a win. In the bright sunny glow of consistent wins. I had a client once who complained about her manager's resistance to her request for fast-tracked development toward a next-level role. Needing a bit of information to help me construct a strategy, I said, "Tell me about your current performance." *Uh. Err. Umm. Well... See, what had happened was...* What tumbled from my client's mouth was all of the excuses and reasons why she had missed deadlines, or turned in subpar work, or was not meeting her goals.

I remember pausing and tilting my head to the side, like dogs do, because I was not sure if I had heard her correctly. *Was she seriously asking why her boss wouldn't be in the mood to help her grow to the next level when she was failing to perform where she was?* I'll say it as plainly now as I tried to then: there is no moving to the next level if you are not delivering where you are now. It's so important, it bears repeating: there is no moving to the next level if you are not delivering where you are now. For the people in the back row: there is no moving to the next level if you are not delivering where you are now.

Continue to deliver value for your boss, matrixed managers, direct reports, peers, partners, and internal or external customers. Continue to nurture and evidence your leadership brand. Continue to learn the nuances of leadership at different levels. Continue to walk the path, but stay present. Seed your dream, but not at the detriment of competently attending to what is in front of you, now, here, in your current role. Nothing will put a pin in your next-level balloon faster than failing to deliver in your current reality in favor of your future aspiration. Abandon your *now* and you will kill off your *next*.

A Word on Confidence

Confidence, like the word *leadership*, resists definition. But again, like leadership, we know confidence when we see it in others and feel it within ourselves. We know confidence is magnetic, drawing opportunity to the person it inhabits. Confidence steels the spine, fortifying the leader amid the toss and tumult of stormy circumstance. Amid all the activity and strategy and awareness-raising I advocate in this book, underneath it all must be the constant hum of confidence. We know what confidence is not. Arrogance. Entitlement. Impatience. Like the fawney brass rings of common street hustlers, confidence has many imposters. These will not serve you. They are not the trappings of leadership. They are fakes. But how do you discern confidence from the counterfeit?

Again it comes down to value-add, and you recognizing what yours uniquely is. It's knowing the nature of your own superpower. Your secret sauce. Your most consistent strength. The unique thing you bring to the work, through which you cause positive change. You must know it—like you know you have a heart in your chest and a brain in your head.

There is a biblical passage that says: "Faith without works is dead." But *works*, as it is used here, I think, has a dual meaning. Firstly, the *work* the passage is talking about is the work of exercising, developing, and practicing your value-add. *Work* describes the care and feeding of this most valuable attribute. We *work* a thing because we prize it. We take care of it. We nurture it. Athletes *work* their muscles. Scholars *work* their intellect. Vocalists *work* their range, and writers, to *work* their craft, write every day.

What follows work is belief. The athlete *believes* in his muscles. The scholar *believes* in her intellect. The vocalist *believes* in his range, and the writer *believes* in her craft. This belief, however, isn't a blind belief; it's built on the *work* they have invested. And because they have *worked* their value-add, they can confidently put their value-add to work. Here, I think, *work* morphs to mean performance. Here is where the value-add you have worked and exercised can be set loose to perform. Have you enough faith in your value-add to try its performance? Are you willing to road test and rely on it? Do you trust it enough to put it through its paces and bet on it winning? For your value-add to manifest in ways that will fuel your next-level aspirations, you must *work it* (develop it, practice it) enough to *work it* (test its performance) and lean on it in real time—because you know, without doubt, it's there, and thus, can be trusted to deliver.

"A bird sitting in a tree is never afraid of the branch breaking because its trust is—not in the branch, but in its own wings." This passage by an unknown author says it so poetically. The bird doesn't trust the branch. It trusts its own tried and true wings. Don't trust the branch. When you recognize, exercise, develop, and believe in your value-add, you can trust your own tried and true wings.

An Insider Tip
When You Don't Know What to Believe

Instead of struggling to identify which of your strengths deserve your belief and actionable trust, here are two exercises that can help bring the answers to the surface.

Archive Your Wins. As you achieve in big and small ways at work, keep a record. Perhaps it's a file, a journal, or a scrapbook. Whatever it is, collect the evidence of your wins. When you stumble and forget why you are on this road, and on it for good reason, pull out this archive to remind yourself.

Study Your Wins. At the close of a complex project, many organizations and work groups perform a lessons-learned session or an autopsy of the work. The practice involves looking over the process for its weaknesses and missteps. The hope is that if those things can be identified, they are mistakes the group can avoid or mitigate with more intention the next time. Holding a lessons-learned session is a strategic best practice, but many people often only focus on what went wrong. When you win, study it for what went right, for the same purpose: so that you can repeat the strengths, with intention, the next time.

For example, identify the last several projects or assignments where you delivered well. For each project, identify three to five steps, actions, or choices of yours that proved essential to the positive outcome. After examining your most *recent assignments in this manner, it is highly likely a pattern will emerge. There are probably things you do repeatedly, assignment to assignment, that help result in a good outcome. Analyze and identify what this secret sauce is so that you can repeat it with intention next time.*

Confidence is not a magic panacea or cure-all, though. Belief in yourself doesn't make you immune to life's slings and arrows; it means you trust that your strengths will help you achieve despite them. Belief in yourself will not make you impervious to disappointments, but trusting your strengths will enable you to navigate through them. Stepping out of your comfort zone is hard and frightening; belief in yourself doesn't change that. But trusting that your abilities will kick in once you're deep in the unknown, will. Confidence does not mean you are free of fear and failure. It simply means you trust your value-add enough to know that you won't just recover, you will also once again, fly.

Getting Started

I'm fanatical about getting oil changes for my vehicle. As someone who dreads the idea of being stuck and stranded on some dark and solitary highway, mechanical preventative maintenance is my string of garlic to stave off my dark and bloodthirsty road-worries. Maintaining your car is critical to its longevity and, as someone who has seen way too many horror movies, to my peace of mind as I travel from here to there. En route to the next level, keep your vehicle well maintained. Strategic patience is not passivity—quite the opposite. Strategic patience is about actively keeping your value-add well oiled and prepared for when lightning strikes. Whether it's keeping your relationships in good shape or dissecting your wins, use your *meantime* to get ready for when the time is right.

Chapter 12

THE NINE, ANSWERED

Unsticking stuck and suspended careers

IT'S TIME TO sew up something I have left undone. You remember them, the Nine, who were stuck in careers in suspended animation. When we last saw them, the people in these scenarios were struggling to reveal themselves as ready to cause positive change in their organizations. They were floundering in situational quicksand, a clear marker that their leadership capability was vulnerable to the risk of being hidden in plain sight. Now, it's time they set themselves free. It's time for them to unlock the leaders they really are. They just need a little coaching. And I'm happy to oblige. Meanwhile, be a fly on the wall as I coach each leader through his or her specific problem. Pay attention to the real-life application of the concepts we have discussed. But also keep an eye out for a few new bonus gems I have thrown in just for fun.

Overpass'd

You went for it—the senior management role—just as you've done before, thinking surely this time would be different. Then they gave it to someone else with qualifications equal to your own. And if that wasn't painful enough, this marks the third time you've been passed over... and over... and over.

Overpass'd, you sense that something's wrong. Although you don't know what is blocking your pursuit of what you want, you sense that something is clearly off, and you're right. Something *is* wrong, and that's bad enough. But what's worse is that you don't know what it is. You haven't stopped to learn what the problem is, and so long as you stay in the dark about what's getting in your way, in the face of a clear pattern, the more rapidly your predicament moves away from being a sympathetic and unfortunate event, to being purely willful blindness.

To unlock your leadership, apply these visible competencies:

- Learn and course correct as new data emerges.

- Regularly engage in activities that provide insights and feedback to broaden self-knowledge.

- Maintain focus, endurance, resilience, and sound judgment during delay, change, ambiguity, stress, or crisis.

There's that often used assertion that doing the same thing over and over and expecting a different result is insanity. In this case, it's insane because what you're doing has repeatedly failed to produce a result, yet still, even in the face of this clear data, you keep expecting something else to happen. Overpass'd, it's time to step away from crazy! Stop waiting for something different to occur when you have done nothing different to facilitate the change you want to see. Now it's time to do something else. Here I go, quoting my mother again: "Do the same, get the same." Put another way: "Nothing will change until you change it." All of these truisms are speaking to the state of churning, in which you are miserably caught. They are all begging that you add new data to this turning wheel of same bad action, same bad result, same bad action, same bad result. New information will interrupt this spinning that's taking you nowhere fast—or slow for that matter. What's the new information? Feedback.

If possible, ask the interviewer about what, in your interview answers or presentation, is working and what is not—and it's important to get both. By just getting the *what's working*, you protect your ego from the sting of your own frailties, and you also destine yourself to repeat the same mistakes. By just getting what's not working, you amply punish yourself with your limitations, but you also never learn what's serving you and what to repeat. Perhaps it's something you're saying or doing in the interview. Perhaps you lack a particular competency. Perhaps it's something in your reputation that precedes you. Perhaps it's a full moon. Perhaps it's… You could go on and on, supposing it's this or that. You can continue guessing, or you can, through feedback, get some new data and, along with it, many different choices and options besides repeating what is clearly not working.

If getting feedback is not an option, here's another strategy that may help you get to the same destination. Consider each of your last several interviews. For each one, make a list of three to five actions, statements, or decisions you made that seem to bode well and not so well. Conduct this exercise for each interview. When you have finished, it is likely that you will see patterns emerging: patterns of what works and patterns around what doesn't work. If you are unsure which behaviors are working or not, take these patterns to a trusted manager, coach, or mentor to get an opinion. Getting feedback can sting. Although averting it buys the avoidance of pain, it also buys ignorance and the futility of perpetually spinning your wheels.

Overpass'd, there's another element to this we should discuss. When we experience rejection upon rejection, it's easy to want to look outside of ourselves for the cause, even going as far as to wonder if some nefarious "-ism," such as racism, sexism, or ageism, is at play. That's a possibility. Employment discrimination is real and occurs when an employee is treated unfavorably on the basis of race, skin color, national origin, gender, disability, religion, or age. It is illegal to discriminate in any facet of employment, including hiring, firing, and promotion. Although discrimination via retaliation—committing illegal employment practices as a way of punishing an employee who has engaged in legally protected activity—accounts or is included in almost half of all charges filed, the US Equal Employment Opportunity Commission (EEOC) also cites the following as types of employment discrimination allegedly occurring in the 2017 fiscal year:

- Race: 28,528 (33.9%)

- Disability: 26,838 (31.9%)

- Sex: 25,605 (30.4%)

- Age: 18,376 (21.8%)

- National origin: 8,299 (9.8%)

- Religion: 3,436 (4.1%)

- Color: 3,240 (3.8%)

These percentages add up to more than 100% because some charges allege multiple issues. In 2017, the EEOC achieved a successful outcome in 91% of resolutions.[24] If you suspect that this kind of employment discrimination is occurring, the EEOC in your local municipality can assist you in bringing an investigation.

When I have encountered clients who alleged discrimination as the cause of their career's immobility, I don't doubt what they are experiencing. But I am also slow to press that big red button. Discrimination is outside of your control, whereas your performance is within it. Giving power over to something outside of themselves feels like I am infantilizing my clients when, in truth, I see them as powerful. I encourage an exploration of the vulnerabilities that may exist in my client's performance or brand first. In my experience as a seasoned HRian, most of the time, most of what ailed my clients' career trajectory was inside them.

Finally, I wanted to say a little something about brand—specifically, the one you are building. Applying, and applying, and applying for jobs, especially if these roles are in a variety of different disciplines, begins to tell a story of someone who will take anything. It tells a story of someone who is running from something instead of toward it. It starts to look like you're throwing a bowl of delicious pasta carbonara—with wonderful pancetta and fresh peas—against the wall to see what will stick. It's a tragic end for such a wonderful meal, and it's not so good as a career-building strategy either. Overapplying reeks of desperation and not the kind of scent you want following you into your next interview. To review:

- Repeated rejections signal the need for feedback to learn what is getting in your way.

- The EEOC can assist with credible allegations of employment discrimination.

- Repetitive applying can negatively impact your brand.

In Time Out

You said the words: "I want to be developed..." You asked because you are ready to take the reins to advance your career. You'll take whatever tools and training your boss will offer. What's not clear is whether your boss is taking you seriously, but what is clear, by the fact that nothing's happened, is that your boss is taking his own sweet time.

In Time Out, sometimes we fail to get what we need because we don't help people to *help us.* To the fact that you asked for your manager's partnership along your development journey, I say: bravo! In organizations, nothing of any significance gets done in isolation, including your development as a leader. Some would have sat passively waiting for an invitation that, for most, never comes. No one can psychically know your wants and needs, so asking for what you want is always wise. Your approach to asking, on the other hand, not so much.

When you went into your manager's office and asked for development, you essentially dumped not one, but two big problems into your boss' lap. The first problem you generously bestowed was the challenge of mind reading what you meant by "develop me..." The second problem was leaving whatever "develop me..." means up to your manager to put into an actionable strategy. You've left your boss to figure out both the *what* and the *how*. Ambiguous requests that make a manager guess are nothing but, to a manager's eye, more work. So it should come as no surprise that these kinds of requests generally get low or no priority on a busy manager's ever-present to-do list.

To unlock your leadership, apply these visible competencies:

- Build a clear and realistic vision of the future state of the business.

- Create a compelling case that inspires partnership, alignment, cooperation, action, and followership.

- Create, differentiate, and balance applying strategic versus tactical approaches to meet goals.

In Time Out, you must know what you want so that when the opportunity presents itself, you can make it plain to whoever is listening. When you say *development*, what do you mean? Develop what, exactly? And if you get the development you want, what value will it add to the business?

In Time Out, here's a different approach. Go back and ask for development on a particular issue or behavior, and state the value the developed skill can bring to the group. "I'd like to start learning how to run meetings more effectively so that I can make them more productive and a better use of everyone's time" is much more concrete and achievable than a blanket "Develop me..." In this example, you have given your manager the *what* and the *why*.

Not only should you go back to your manager with a more specific request, but you should also go equipped with a suggestion as to the process by which you can get the exposure or practice you need. This new approach, then, starts with the *what*, turning "Develop me..." into "I'd like to start learning how to run meetings more effectively so that I can make them more productive and a better use of everyone's time." And then it adds a *how*: "Perhaps you could listen in as I conduct a conference call meeting and give me some feedback afterward."

It's easier to edit than it is to design. By that, I mean that even if your manager doesn't like the *how* you suggest—in this case, observing you lead a conference call—it is much easier for your manager to reshape an idea from *something* than to invent an idea from *nothing*. If your manager doesn't like your *how* and suggests something else, so what! What's important is that it signals that you're past getting permission and are now problem solving. And that, in turn, suggests your manager is engaged in trying to meet your needs.

In Time Out, there's one more thing I'd suggest: have a plan B in your back pocket. We left off with plan A: "Perhaps you could listen in as I conduct a conference call meeting and give me some feedback afterward." Now add a plan B, an alternative *how*: "Or, if you don't have time for that, I've noticed Khalil is really strong at running meetings. Would you mind if I asked him for feedback and a few tips?" Here, you offer yet another option relative to the development you want. Initially, you made a request and heard crickets. Help your manager *help you* by providing a *what*, *why*, *how*, and a backup plan. To review:

- Fuzzy and unclear requests often get low or no priority.

- Know specifically what you want, why, and what value it will bring to you and others.

- Come equipped with a suggestion as to a method or strategy, as well as a plan B, an alternative way to meet your goal.

Battlefield Promotion

They threw you into a leadership role during a crisis. It was hard-fought, bloody, and took a lot of work, but you got things back on track and back to normal. But although you've not changed a thing, now they have concerns? Now they're unsure if you can lead?

Battlefield Promotion, although some things may be back to normal, your job isn't one of them. It's changed. It may not have come with a formal application process or a new title, but you are now being called upon to perform a very different job than you were during the crisis. Consider the skill set required of someone leading amid an emergency: sharp thinking, working with urgency and endurance, relentless tenacity, driving for execution, laser focus, cutting through the noise, quick action, and instantly prioritizing the most important things. As evidenced by your success, you clearly exhibited the skills to pull the team to the other side of its predicament. However, now that the circumstance has normalized, what will be required of you strategically, relationally, and relative to how you self-manage is likely a very different list of characteristics.

To unlock your leadership, apply these visible competencies:

- Read the situation to inform the appropriateness of what to do or say next.

- Express passion, enthusiasm, and energy appropriate to the circumstance.

- Learn and course correct as new data emerges.

Earlier, we considered Jacob, the client specialist in customer service who found himself at a point where he needed to decide what he could and could not afford to do to maintain his reputation as a coolheaded professional. It appears as if Jacob chose wisely, behaving in ways that supported how he wanted to be perceived. But then we pulled Jacob out of his customer service chair and put him smack dab in the middle of an inferno, with people in need of rescue. Battlefield Promotion, leadership is about managing and manifesting your best self so that you can influence others, with and through whom you must cause change and add value. Although an accommodating, gentle, and affable manner was Jacob's best on the phone with his customer, would that same manner be Jacob at his best among the flames? Doubtful.

Your best self when the sky is falling is likely very different from your best self when the sky is blue and filled with sunshine—or at least, it should be. You in a crisis shouldn't be you when no crisis exists. Being a leader and your best self means knowing what parts of you to summon and what other parts to still per the given environment. You were your best self during the crisis, using the skills and characteristics that situation required. However, now the crisis has abated; what would be the characteristics of your best self now that things are calm?

Battlefield Promotion, you mentioned not changing a thing. Armed with what you know now, can you see how that should have been your red flag? Different circumstances require a different assortment of skills. You will need to activate different parts of yourself to prove effective in what is now a very different job—a job that requires a very different version of you. To review:

- Changing conditions at work need your versatility.

- Your best self in one circumstance may not prove best in all cases.

- Evaluate what each situation requires; then summon the appropriate parts of you to meet them.

Hamster Wheel

You want a management role. But you're not going to get it without experience. That's why you need the management role, which you can't get without the experience. How are you supposed to get experience without a management role, which would give you experience for the management role you want?

Hamster Wheel, I'll meet you halfway. I'll acknowledge your righteous frustration. It's like being caught in a perpetual state of churning. You're on a Möbius strip where potential movement recycles upon itself, resulting in no real movement at all; talk about stuck! Again, I can acknowledge that, but only if you can recognize the extravagance of your request.

To unlock your leadership, apply these visible competencies:

- Embrace development opportunities and experiences that encourage learning and skill growth.

- Cooperate toward outcomes that offer mutual benefit.

- Execute plans, emphasizing the activities that matter most.

Yes, I said *extravagant*. For you, the ideal experience would be a paid and full-time training opportunity at the helm of your very own team. But for your manager, that would translate into a full-time and fully compensated tryout of an untested individual with an unsuspecting team of real people who need and deserve real leadership. What you want is tantamount to an expensive social experiment with unpredictable impacts on the business and its people. Let me be clear; the heart of what you want is perfectly reasonable: experience and practice leading. The *how* you have suggested is not. The process you've proposed is full of complexity, permanence, and risk. It situates you in a real position, with real business implications, with a real salary change, and managing real people who have real problems and needs.

Let's focus for a moment on your *how*, which, without the training and experience, activates a myriad of systemic, business, and human resource challenges. Is all of that really necessary to give you what you want, especially if we home in on the *what*? I mean the real *what*: you getting experience and practice leading. How can your manager test your leadership in ways that are mutually beneficial without your manager, the business, and other employees taking a risk? The answer is stretch assignments.

Hamster Wheel, yours is the dilemma of someone who is narrowly defining how to acquire experience. When most say the word "experience", what they mean is a practical education—that is, knowledge that is actionable and that can be practiced, exercised and, finally, applied in a real circumstance that is organic and unpredictable (unlike the highly controlled and artificial situations you might get in a training class). So let's be clear: what you want is experience. However, what you're asking for is a promotion. That's unreasonable, especially if it is only the means to an end that could be had in a variety of other, less impactful ways.

There are many ways to ask for and acquire practical knowledge without promoting you, which any manager might find too tall, complicated, and risky an order. In partnership with your boss, identify assignments that will involve social leadership without attaching the formal authority that usually goes with it. It doesn't matter what the project is as long as it tests your ability to drive change that adds value with and through other people. Start with projects that are low risk and low visibility. Identify tasks that only involve a few people or a small team. Along the way, engage your manager as a coach, and get feedback you can integrate and use. During check-ins with your boss, discuss how you are incorporating his or her feedback and what happens as a result.

As you gain experience, ask your manager to turn up the risk, the visibility, and the number of people involved. This strategy not only builds a repertoire of experiences, but it also situates your manager to witness you successfully and repeatedly leading in an increasingly larger context over an extended period of time. To review:

- Evaluate and reduce the risk your development request poses to the people whose support you need.

- Start small, and raise the stakes over time.

- Engage your manager in coaching you and witnessing your growth.

Stuck on Assistant

You're already in management—well, sort of. You're an assistant supervisor, an invisible and meaningless title, with no real authority unless the boss is on vacation. And even then, when it comes to their questions or concerns, the staff members say they'll just wait 'til the boss is back. Getting your manager and others to see you as a full-fledged leader seems so out of reach— 'cause all they see when they look at you is the assistant, the right-hand, the second in command—never the one in charge.

Stuck on Assistant, there is a body of professional development called Dress-For-Success work. It focuses on polishing the exterior look of a person as a way of building his or her inner confidence. In that work, you'll often hear the phrase, "Don't dress for the position you have; dress for the position you want." This is the concept of leading according to context, simply applied to pantsuits. If you want to be seen as an upper-level leader, you have to, whenever possible, demonstrate upper-level leadership.

To unlock your leadership, apply these visible competencies:

- Be flexible to the needs of others and variable situations while remaining authentic.

- Be intentional and operate with purpose.

- Anticipate and prepare for future changes.

You know all leadership competency behaviors manifest in the contexts of leading self, others, and business. Stuck on Assistant, let's examine one competency that will likely be expected in the role you want: *creating strategic approaches and action plans that drive change*. Look closer at it, and focus on what is at its core: change—specifically, driving change through practical strategies and plans. Now consider how this single competency changes in different contexts and evolves as you climb from one level to another.

An individual contributor or a leader of self, for example, will most likely be expected to adapt to and execute change strategies that come down from leaders up above. An individual contributor will be evaluated on his or her ability to self-manage and maintain effectiveness during the transition from the current state to the changed state.

Meanwhile, what's expected of a leader of others or a people manager will be entirely different. Generally, when you are a people manager, you are not executing. You are an enabler, clearing the way and providing the resources so that others can perform. It's not about what you can execute but the extent to which you can help others. A leader of others would be expected to see change coming and to help the team prepare for it. A people manager would need to be able to delegate tasks, coach, and support the team through the transition, as well as help normalize conditions when the team reaches the other side.

Stuck on Assistant, as a senior leader or a leader of business who is likely responsible for several teams or large-scale strategic initiatives, you are neither an enabler nor the person who executes a task. At this level, you are the strategist. Now, the expectation is for you to anticipate and drive large-scale change or change that positively impacts the whole organization. Activities at this level may also include building an enterprise vision that the people leaders, in turn, translate into more local objectives and plans of action for the individual contributors, who will ultimately carry them out.

In each context, the expectation around the ability to drive change through practical strategies doesn't shift; how it uniquely manifests does. Stuck on Assistant, currently, you sit in a position that puts you between an individual contributor and full-scale people management. If you want to climb contexts, first get clear on how the expression of a competency changes from the assistant supervisor level to the manager level. Next, ask for stretch assignments that allow you to learn the nuances that differentiate one role from the other. Then, make the behaviors and abilities in this gap the focus of your development strategy. Finally, ask your manager for guardrails to keep you challenged and growing, while also keeping you from going too far outside of range and into territory your current leadership profile cannot support. To review:

- Focus on the contextual differences between the role you have and the role you want.

- Investigate how a competency is demonstrated

differently from level to level and target those behaviors in your development plan.

- Get your manager's support and guidance to keep you challenged but within scope.

Fallen Star

Before this, all you had to worry about was playing your best game. So that's what you did, and that's why your bosses bumped you up into management. Now you're in the penalty box for not doing your job? Being the star player got you in the arena. So why does it seem that to stay in the spotlight, you will have to be something other than what put you there?

Fallen Star, you just hit it out of the park; they *do* want you to be something else: not a star but a star-maker. Let's look at a replay to understand what has happened—because it frequently happens to MVPs just like you. Whatever you were, it shone brightly and was likely very valued indeed. The *theys*, recognizing a star player when they see one, suddenly have cloning on their minds; yes, cloning. To replicate the strengths the *theys* value, stars like you are frequently promoted to leadership roles. And there's where the game plan often falls apart.

Stars are frequently promoted without regard to whether those players know how to or want to become leaders. So focused on duplicating the skills of the promoted, the *theys* often forget that being a star is not the same as being a star-maker. Being a top player is not the same as being a coach. Being a great individual contributor is not the same as being a manager. What starts as a winning proposition for both the employee and the organization, ends up being a situation that can set talented employees up to fail, after being thrown into jobs for which they are not prepared.

To unlock your leadership, apply these visible competencies:

- Regularly engage in activities that provide insights and feedback to broaden self-knowledge.

- Learn and course correct as new data emerges.

- Embrace development opportunities and experiences that encourage learning and skill growth.

In this situation, self-awareness is vital. Fallen Star, had you, at the time you took the promotion, been armed with the insights you have now, you may have concluded that a next-level role or formal promotion was not for you. Although you enjoyed being the star on the court, growing star quality in others wasn't necessarily part of your game. If we could go back in time, Fallen Star, you may have decided against people management. But would that have been OK? The answer depends on what you can afford. With every choice comes rewards and consequences. However, when you base a decision on having measured what saying no to an opportunity buys and costs, and whether it is something you can or want to afford, at the very least, you are demonstrating strong self-leadership, and that's a must, no matter what you choose.

If you choose to evolve into the new position of star-maker, like Battlefield Promotion, know that the situation is indeed different. You were a leader of self. Now you must be a leader of others, which is a wholly different game. An individual contributor's lens can be narrow and concerned with those things that only impact the contributor's own job. As a leader of people, that lens needs to widen. Your job is no longer about focusing on your own star moves; now the job is to teach those moves to others. And whether or not you have successfully made the transition from player to coach can be seen even in the smallest and seemingly insignificant ways.

One of my clients, whose story initially inspired this book, learned this the hard way. He came to me still smarting over a recent loss of a job opportunity he really wanted. He and his lone competitor were nearly equally matched as they vied for the role of director of sales, and in some ways, résumé-wise, my client was even stronger. But I would learn from the executive hiring manager that it wasn't the presence of the alphabet soup of abbreviated degrees after my client's name that mattered. It was the small pronouns he used—*my, I,* and *me*—that dulled his edge compared to his contender. Whereas my client concentrated on his own impressive sales record, his competitor's focus, the hiring manager shared, was significantly more oriented to the team: "*our* vision as a *team*"; "the goals *we* as a *team* will pursue"; "nothing can stop *us* as a *team,* if *we* work *together.*" *Our, we, team, us, together*— those small words made all the difference relative to a role where success rested on teamwork. My client had proven he was a superior leader—of self. However, as his own words reflected, his evident readiness to lead others came up short.

Fallen Star, to be a winner, making the transition from employee to manager will be vital to your success. When people fail to make the shift between player and coach, they often end up competing with their own employees. They favor what serves themselves, as individuals, versus what helps the group. They remain doers instead of becoming enablers. Your leadership walk and talk must shift just like your position has. Making the move to your new role may require new skills and thus more training. You know how to be a star player; you may need to learn how to be a coach and a leader of people. To review:

- A move from individual contributor to people manager, even when it happens in the same work group, is a completely different role.

- Using the same approach in a new position is usually a failing strategy.

- Get the development and training resources you need to be effective in the new job.

Out of Sight

You've kept your head down, your nose to the grindstone, pumping out good work, because sooner or later, someone's got to take notice. You've built the right skills, got the right experience, and displayed it all beautifully on the right résumé. It's everything that should help your leadership qualities stand out, loud and proud, except for the fact that no one's looking.

Out of Sight, it likely begins in high school, the encouragement to capture your employment and career value in a résumé. In college and out in the workforce, the need for résumés, a strong social media presence, and other forms of personal marketing are reinforced, and for good reason. In our digitally networked world, people and organizations will run a search in an effort to *know you* virtually, even when, and sometimes especially when, they anticipate meeting you IRL, in real life. And we play along. We capture our story in a one-sheet résumé or in an online profile in hopes of influencing people we will meet much later or never meet IRL at all. However, once you're inside of an organization, all that changes a bit. To unlock your leadership, apply these visible competencies:

- Create wins, advantages, or solutions for customers and other stakeholders.

- Continuously drive for results.

- Build your expertise and brand as a reliable partner, credible manager, or trusted adviser.

Once you're inside an organization, the influencing power of your résumé declines. Once inside, the résumé's ability to paint a picture of you is not as compelling as it was when you were an outsider. Now that you are part of the family, the résumé can quickly demonstrate that you meet the list of qualifications, but what it cannot supersede is your internal brand and reputation. The résumé won't power your leadership journey within the enterprise; only your reputational value, visibility, and volume will do that.

What in the organization changes for the better as a result of you being there? The answer is your value. As we have discussed, your value must flow beyond yourself and into the group, into the team, to your manager, to the strategic focus of your department, or into the enterprise as a whole. Your value must be increasingly discernible if it is to act as proof of your readiness to lead or lead at a higher level. Ideally, your value-add is visible and can be described as quantifiable or expressed as increasing and decreasing something of significance in the business. Value can also be expressed through anecdotes and stories if you focus on the cause and positive effect between your actions and positive business outcomes. These depictions of your value, whether in number, percentage, or story form, must visibly demonstrate that your organization is better as a result of you being there.

Finally, add this visible value generously—at every opportunity—*in volume*, that is, as much and as often as you can. It should become what you are known for; it should become just what you do. Adding visible value in ways that are unique to you builds your reputation and brand. Some people don't have to seek out opportunities because opportunity finds them. Some people command and attract big breaks. Some people get tapped for a chance at something great without the need for a résumé because their reputation *is* their résumé. Make it yours as well. To review:

- Once inside an organization, résumés lose their impact. Your internal reputation accounts for more.

- Seek to add value that is visible and can be measured.

- Add value in volume and generously, embedding it into your reputation.

Untitled

They have all sorts of names for what you are: workhorse, worker bee, B player. But although all of them sound so commendable, what you really are is a seasoned specialist with a lot of experience and deep insight into what you do. You want them to see you as a specialized knowledge

expert and thought leader—not just a solid performer,
but their trusted, go-to person.

Untitled, instead of worrying about what they call you, worry about your brand and the value you add. Like Out of Sight, your problem isn't what you can do; it's that no one knows it. Yours is a problem of visibility or, more to the point, invisibility. Raising your profile as a subject-matter expert isn't hard, but it will take time, strategy, and generosity. To unlock your leadership, apply these visible competencies:

- Study trends and the future business landscape, while interpreting the implications.

- Help key stakeholders respond strategically to what you have observed or recommended.

- Build your expertise and brand as a reliable partner, credible manager, or trusted adviser.

If you want to be known as a knowledge expert or thought leader, first become a thought follower, a committed student of the subject matter that fascinates you. But be selective. The difference between having an interesting pastime and being a relevant thought leader is that the latter is fascinated with subjects that help solve the real problems real people have in the workplace. If you know a lot about something that no one needs, that may be an interesting hobby, but little more than that. Thought leadership, like plain ol' leadership, is about creating an improved end state. It's about causing a change that adds value. It's about solving a problem or grabbing an opportunity that will change the way things are for the better. Although most SMEs are in love with their area of expertise, there is something they love even more: the problems they can solve.

Many think being a thought leader means dispensing useful information, and it does, but not before being a learner. SMEs are voracious consumers of data, studies, models, techniques, and innovations relative to their area of interest. They study what they love without getting paid for it and without it being assigned to them. Also, as a way of taking in information, SMEs are great listeners, seeking to understand the gaps, the problems, along with the pain their internal clients are feeling. Listening is what helps the SME bring back not just any solution, but a solution that fits the problem like a glove. As someone who embraced her inner nerd long ago, let me give it to you straight: if your expertise isn't married to a practical business problem you can help someone solve, you're not an SME; you're a tinkerer who's just *nerding out* with an interesting diversion.

Finally, be generous with it. Give it away. At every opportunity, offer your quality solutions and insights so consistently that your focus area becomes your brand and tied to your name in the organization. Do it so consistently that when people think of that challenge and whom they need to call to fix it, they think of you. As you increasingly get invited to solve problems, measure the impact of the expertise and thought leadership you provide. What increases or decreases when you apply your thinking as a solution? When an internal client uses what you know, follow up to learn the outcomes. These outcomes can become examples, case studies, and the core of storytelling that demonstrates the value you bring. To review:

- Become a student of your area of interest and the problems you solve.

- Turn what you know into pragmatic and usable solutions of value.

- Be generous with the value you provide until it becomes associated with who you are.

Golden Cage

Besides being really good at what you do, you're a rare bird with a unique and high-value set of skills. But when it's time to fly to the next level, they clip your wings. They want you where you are, laying your golden eggs. Leaving the company? Not an option; you have a lot invested. But there's no getting over the irony: what they most respect and reward in you is the very thing keeping you caged.

Golden Cage, the fault of what you're experiencing rests in large part with your manager. There is no kind way to say it: your manager is a hoarder of good talent. Your manager can clearly see your undeniable gifts while also being simultaneously shortsighted in more ways than one. Yours is a manager who is choosing his or her needs over the health and well-being of the enterprise that would, in the event of you moving up or even over into another department, still get the benefit of your unique value-add. Hoarding managers risk the organization's ability to retain its top talent.

Talent hoarding also casts light onto a manager's poor planning relative to employee development. You want to move up, but it could have just as easily been the case that you hit the lottery and decided to move to the Fiji Islands. Or perhaps you had the unfortunate luck of being kidnapped by clowns. Whatever your demise or opportunity, what was your manager's plan B?

A stronger leader, guided by the fact that nothing lasts forever, would have developed others with the same or similar skills so that no one employee's voluntary or involuntary separation would have such a devastating impact on the organization's brain and talent stores. Shame on your manager for putting you in a position to pay for his or her missteps. To unlock your leadership, apply these visible competencies:

- Develop others toward growth and achievement.

- Stimulate results by leveraging best and next practice, strategic tools, and technologies.

- Help people transition to the new normal.

Although I chastised your manager, I also have a few words for you, Golden Cage: a reality check. If cruel, know that it is only to kindly remind you that what you are experiencing is not your imagination, nor is it something to take personally. Remember that more than benefitting the employee, job placements, including promotions, are rooted in two primary motivators: the surviving and thriving of the organization. Keeping you in place may only be a strategic play in the interest of the enterprise. You must also consider the fact that promoted roles don't come cheap. For every rung on the career ladder you successfully climb, you leave open positions to fill in your wake. Even when the organization promotes its internal talent, job backfilling can cost 33% of the open position's salary, factoring in not only salary jumps, but also the time ramping up the promoted employees to full functionality in their new roles. Golden Cage, what you want costs. Although there is a path toward your goal, that will cost you too: strategic planning.

Implementing this strategy requires Newtonian consideration, the economy of choice, and managing the principles of cause and effect. Taking the path toward your increased promotability will undoubtedly buy you the opportunity to climb. But it will cost, and like all things, you'll have to decide if you can afford it. The first cost is self-managing. The frustration you may feel is completely justified. Usually expertise, skills, talents, energy, and efforts like yours are the drivers of growth, not stuckness. But don't let the current circumstance get in your way or worse, burrow itself deep down to infect your attitude and performance. Instead, I invite you to reframe what's happening to you. And what's happening is that there is a high premium on the value you uniquely add. Try to see the flattery in it. What you bring to the business is gold; and, your manager's only human. Who wouldn't want to keep a prize like you all to themselves?

The second cost is political. Your manager sees your ascending flight as a threat. You must work to reduce this anxiety. Although that is not on your job description, your manager can be among the most influential advocates of your growth in the organization. It is imperative that you remain his or her closely aligned partner in advancing business outcomes, so keep yourself in your manager's good graces and on task.

Your manager's empire remains at risk and vulnerable even with your engagement and partnership. That's because the strength of your boss' strategic hand relies on a single ace: you. You can help your manager reduce that risk, but be warned: doing so, Golden Cage, will cost you as well. Here's what you are buying: your manager feeling comfortable enough to set you free. Here's what that might cost: you must do what your manager hasn't, and that is multiplying the sources of your specialized knowledge.

You must help grow and develop a junior SME like you, or systems by which your manager can access the intelligence and brain trust your specialized knowledge represents. It's not fair that you will have to do part of your manager's job for him or her, but life, in or out of organizations, isn't always fair. And sometimes people have to pay more than full freight to fly. The price for you is demonstrating specific practices of a leader or manager well before the *theys* will officially call you one.

Engage your manager as a coach as you, in turn, coach the junior SME. Doing so gives your manager a direct line of sight to the progress you are making. It allows your manager to observe, up close, as you replicate the source of your precious specialty in someone else. If you opt to build a system that houses what you offer, approach it as if you were building it for your manager as his or her consultant. First, ask questions—lots of them. Get a keen understanding of what your boss needs to feel comfortable using a different way of sourcing the data that your manager currently relies on you to provide. To review:

- At the core of this dilemma is the high premium your manager is placing on how you add value.

- Being held back, although not a strong

people-management move, is likely just a strategic one. Don't take it personally.

- Keep delivering and positioning yourself as your manager's partner and resource.

- Find visible ways to replicate in others what your manager sees as accessible only through you.

Getting Started

Although each of the Nine is grappling with his or her own unique dilemma and set of circumstances, they all share at least one thing in common: the need to take ownership of their journey toward next-level leadership. Some elements of that journey are outside of your control. For example, your organization is a closed ecosystem. It has rules, policies, and norms by which all of its inhabitants must abide. The nature of the organization, in which you journey, influences the journey itself. Your manager also has a high degree of control and influence over your situation. As your manager evaluates your effectiveness in your current position and your potential for any future roles, he or she can fuel or slow your movement to the next level.

However, what the Nine have done is underestimate the power of their own choices. They all, in part, abdicate and release the reins of their own upward movement. They leave the necessary momentum to climb in the hands of other people. In this way, all of them are blocking their own aspirations. In this way, all of them have the opportunity to take more ownership over their next-level goals.

Leadership is about causing change and value, with and through others, as inspired through your ability to self-manage. Self-management. It has been at the heart of this entire conversation. Your choice to *do* leadership—and to do it visibly, your choice to do the things that nonleaders don't, and your choice to consistently behave in ways that reflect how you uniquely add value within a variety of contexts—these are the most critical drivers of your next-level success story. And they are entirely within your control. Own that. Own your journey to leadership at the next level. Own your journey toward being the leader you really are.

Conclusion

At its most fundamental, leadership is about you creating a positive change at work and in the world. Your dream of leading or of achieving a higher level of leadership is worthy of your energy, ambition, and your earnest pursuit. Now more than ever, organizations need diverse, enthusiastic, and well-prepared leaders. If that opportunity comes to you, or if you make your way to it, remember, you are your most powerful instrument that can move the will of other people to advance amazing and positive change.

However, your expanded understanding of how leadership works is not enough to put you in the line of sight of those with the power to elevate you into the roles you want. Your actions, and what happens as a result of those actions, must match the needs of the circumstance in which your leadership is expected to show itself. The higher you climb, the more intense and precarious these expectations will get. If you remain keenly aware of the subtle guidance of context, you can convert that tension into fuel. The organization's decision makers, the *theys*, need to see the good you can do, not just once or twice but repeatedly, until those actions become associated with the person they believe you are.

Leader, know this: what you want is achievable, but you must choose to do what leaders do. You must choose to do it out loud and beyond the safety of wishful thinking and your comfort zone. My hope for you is that you choose it. I hope you choose leadership. I hope you choose to be the leader you've always been.

Thank you again for making this book a part of your development journey. I hope you found it a useful tool and supportive of your next-level goals. If so, I invite you to leave a quick and honest review on the site where you purchased it. Your thoughts and feedback are a welcomed gift that helps me deliver my very best.

Working River Leadership Consulting, a northeast Ohio training boutique, designs and delivers business-to-business and business-to-consumer learning products and services for working professionals, managers, and organizational leaders. Our core offerings—leadership management and professional career development, leader craft, executive coaching, mastermind groups, live and online workshops, learning events, and strategic consultation—help us deliver on our mission: to help people walk in their unique brand of leadership in ways that add lasting value to their organizations and themselves. Anchoring this business is the principle of supporting the rise of people who would serve as highly effective leaders in their organizations... leaders who drive results with and through others... leaders who can cause positive change and lasting value... leaders who can serve as a strategic advantage at work.

As the principal of Working River, I invite you to contact us if we can support you further along your leadership journey. Until then, my warmest wishes.

—*Damaris Patterson Price*

www.workingriver.com

Index

D

E

F

G

H

I

J

K

L

Endnotes

1. Chambers et al, 1998

2. Merton, 1948

3. Carroll et al, 1989

4. Plato et al, 2013

5. Carlyle, 1968

6. Spencer, 1873

7. Campbell, 1949

8. Galton, 1892

9. Carlyle, 1968

10. Lewin et al, 1939

11. Hersey et al, 1969

12. EssaysUK.com, 2018

13. Burns, 1979

14. Kotter, 1999

15. Bennis, 2003

16. Peters, 2016

17. Stefoff et al, 2018

18. Kozlowska et al, 2015

19. Shakespeare, 1992

20. Merriman-Webster, n.d.

21. Gramlich, 2019

22. Kelly, 2015

23. Hesselbein, 2000

24. Doyle, 2018

Works Cited

Bennis, Warren G. *On Becoming a Leader: the Leadership Classic*. Oxford: Perseus, 2003.

Burns, James MacGregor. *Leadership*. New York, N.Y: Harper & Row, 1979.

Campbell, Joseph. *The Hero With a Thousand Faces*. Princeton, N.J.: Princeton University Press, 1949.

Carlyle, Thomas. *Carlyle on Heroes, Hero-Worship, and the Heroic in History*. London: Oxford University Press, 1968.

Carroll, Lewis, Richard Croft, and Carol Owen. *Alice's Adventures in Wonderland*. Hong Kong: Oxford University Press, 1989.

Chambers, E.G. & Foulon, Mark & Handfield-Jones, Helen & M. Hankin, Steven & G. Michaels, Edward. *The War for Talent*. The McKinsey Quarterly. 1998.

Doyle, Alison. *Types of Employment Discrimination*. The Balance Careers. 2018. Accessed March 30, 2019. https://www.thebalancecareers. com/types-of-employment-discrimination-with-examples-2060914

Galton, Francis. *Hereditary Genius: an Inquiry into Its Laws and Consequences*. London: Watts & Co., 1892.

Gramlich, John. *10 Facts about Americans and Facebook*. Pew Research Center. Pew Research Center, February 1, 2019. Accessed March 31, 2019. https://www.pewresearch.org/fact-tank/2019/02/01/ facts-about-americans-and-facebook/

Hersey, P. and Blanchard, K.H., *Life Cycle Theory Of Leadership*. Training and Development Journal, 23 (5), 1969.

Hesselbein, Frances, Marshall Goldsmith, and Richard Beckhard. *Organization of the Future*. San Francisco, CA: Jossey-Bass, 2000.

Kelly, Matthew. *The Rhythm of Life: Living Every Day with Passion and Purpose*. North Palm Beach, FL: Beacon, 2015.

Kotter, John P., 1947-. *John P. Kotter On What Leaders Really Do*. Boston :Harvard Business School Press, 1999.

Kozlowska, Kasia, Peter Walker, Loyola Mclean, and Pascal Carrive. *Fear and the Defense Cascade*. Harvard Review of Psychiatry 23, no. 4 (2015). Accessed March 31, 2019. https://doi.org/10.1097/hrp.0000000000000065

Lewin, Kurt, Ronald Lippitt, and Ralph K. White. *Patterns of Aggressive Behavior in Experimentally Created 'Social Climates*. The Journal of Social Psychology 10, no. 2. 1939.

Management and Leadership Principles – Peter F Drucker. UKEssays. com. Accessed March 30, 2019. https://www.ukessays.com/essays/business/management-is-doing-things-right-leadership-is-doing-the-right-things-business-essay.php

Merton, Robert K. *The Self-Fulfilling Prophecy*. The Antioch Review 8, no. 2 (1948).

Peters, Tom. *The Brand Called You*. Fast Company. Fast Company, May 18, 2016. Accessed March 31, 2019. https://www.fastcompany.com/28905/brand-called-you

Phony. Merriam-Webster. Merriam-Webster. Accessed March 31, 2019. https://www.merriam-webster.com/dictionary/phony#note-1

Plato, C. J. Emlyn-Jones, and William Preddy. *Republic*. Cambridge, MA: Harvard University Press, 2013.

Shakespeare, William. *The Tragedy of Hamlet, Prince of Denmark*. New Folger's ed. New York: Washington Square Press/Pocket Books, 1992.

Spencer, Herbert, *The Study of Sociology*. London: Henry S. King, 1873.

Stefoff, Rebecca, Teagan White, and Charles Darwin. *Charles Darwin's On the Origin of Species*. New York: Atheneum Books for Young Readers, 2018.